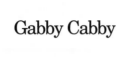

Gabby Cabby

NEW YORK · JOHANNESBURG · CHICAGO · HONG KONG

GABBY CABBY

The Inside Scoop from New York's Last English-Speaking Cabdriver

L. A. · CALGARY · M... ...BLIN · SHANG HAI

Peter Franklin

THE SUMMIT PUBLISHIMG GROUP

THE SUMMIT PUBLISHING GROUP
One Arlington Centre, 1112 East Copeland Road, Fifth Floor
Arlington, Texas 76011
summit@dfw.net
www.summitbooks.com

Printed in the United States of America.

00 99 98 97 96   040   5 4 3 2 1

Library of Congress Cataloging-in-Publication Data
Franklin, Peter, 1948-
    The gabby cabby : the inside scoop from New York's last English
-speaking cab driver / by Peter Franklin.
        p.   cm.
    ISBN 1-56530-223-0
    1. New York (N.Y.)—Social life and customs—Anecdotes.
2. Franklin, Peter, 1948-   —Anecdotes. 3. Taxicabs—New York
(State)—New York—Anecdotes.   I. Title.
    F128.36.F73 1996
    974.7'1—dc20   96-35690
                                                           CIP

Cover and book design by David Sims

Cover Illustration by
Tom Corcoran at Zipatoni and Bill Lux at Hinkle & Company

Illustrations by Nicholas C.D. Franklin

Dedicated to:

Phil Franklin
Mollie Franklin
Chandra Dias
Rohini Dias

who started it all

And to
Alexandria Franklin,
who would have loved
Benjamin, Indy, Dixie, Henry, and Daisy…

Contents

The Forvitz

Once upon a time, there was a newspaper in New York City that was called *The Forvitz*. I am spelling that phonetically because you wouldn't understand it if I wrote it in Yiddish. And, even if you could understand it, what's the difference, since I can't write in Yiddish anyway.

Also, I don't want you to think that I am Jewish because there are a great many people in this world who do not like Jewish people, and I don't want the sales of this book to be hurt by that.

So, for my Jewish readers, I want you to think of me as Peter Friedman. For you gentiles, I will use the name Peter Franklin.

The Forvitz actually meant *The Forward*. It was a wonderful newspaper that captured the spirit of New York City. At some point, the owners of that paper, feeling that there weren't enough people in New York City capable of reading a newspaper that was printed in Yiddish anymore, started printing it in English.

That, my passengers, is the very essence of New York City. It constantly changes and is never the same. You can come here and go home and tell your friends that you saw such and such in The Big Apple. Your friends will tell you that they saw something completely different when they were here. You will all wonder if it is the same city that you are talking about.

I was born here and have lived here all my life, and I still don't believe it. Someday I may figure out how it manages to operate.

I wanted to write a book about my adventures on the streets of New York City, and I wanted it to be not only for people who do come here, but for people who, for one reason or another, may never be able to come here.

There isn't the slightest question in my mind that New York City, in a sense, belongs to every person on the face of the Earth. My story is a way to say hello to you, and now I am your best friend who lives in New York City.

And speaking of best friends, I tell a joke later in this book about people who try to brag about who is the biggest "nothing." Well, I would be the ultimate nothing if it were not for my best friend, Lalina Franklin.

I met her more than two decades ago while I was moving into my first bachelor apartment in Manhattan. She was sitting in front of the building, and I thought that she was the most beautiful person in the world.

Boy, was I right! She turned out to be more than just beautiful in appearance. The woman is beautiful in every possible way. She honored me by marrying me and giving me the three most fantastic children. If it were not for her, I would not have had the wonderful life and the adventures that I have.

In every instance, she has been completely supportive. When I thought I could never write a book, she was there pushing me to do it.

If you enjoy this book, thank her. If you hate it (impossible), blame me.

I also give special thanks to our three children, Nicholas, Catharine, and Alexi, who are my "staff" and help me to pick out the material that I am going to use on my broadcasts.

These are children who are perfect. They eat everything put in front of them. They always do all their homework. Their rooms are always neat. They always go to bed on time. I am sorry that the rest of the world's parents do not have such children.

One other thing. You meet a great many good folks and a great many bad folks in life. I want to tell you about some of the good ones.

I could not have written this book without the friendship of Ric Davis. He went above and beyond the call of duty as a friend, time and time again.

I also want to thank Paul and Rhaylene Britten, and Jeff and Teri Geisenhof and Kirk and Alice Rhone for being there for Lalina when I couldn't be.

And now, I want to thank the Academy...

You Never Know What You Are Going to Pick Up

I t was the best of times, it was the worst of times[1]... and if you don't like that, how about In the beginning[2]...

The day was like all other days driving a taxi on the streets of New York City. It was going from absolute boredom (some passengers just don't have a spark of interest in them) to the wild and wacky that the Big Apple is known for.

But the one event that was to turn me from the role of mild-mannered, shy, introverted, New York City taxi driver into someone who would be known to millions of people all over the world was about to happen.

Let me digress here. If you think for one minute that there is anything about me, or any other New York City taxi driver that is mild mannered, shy, and introverted, then I want to know what sauce you have been putting in your tea.

I just felt that for purposes of literary phrasing, I should claim those attributes. If the truth be known, once I get into my yellow mobile conveyance lounge, I am in reality the

---

[1] *A Tale of Two Cities*; Charles Dickens; Grosset & Dunlap
[2] Genesis 1:1

maestro of the city streets. Or to put it in plain language, your worst nightmare. I never stop talking.

Now don't get me wrong. I am not a bad guy. I am certainly not a bad driver. But, let us not kid ourselves kiddies, being a cabdriver in New York City is not like milking Bessie in Iowa. Even if you weren't a putz, you would have to act like one to survive.

Golly. I have to digress on my digression. I just realized that some of you out-of-towners will not understand the word "putz." At its nicest, it would mean that you are a fool. At its worst, it means that you are that part of the male anatomy that is used for making a pee pee, a wee wee, a number one.

By the way, wonder how a New York City cabdriver makes a pee pee, a wee wee, a number one, in the cab when he can't find a toilet or a tree? Here is a hint. You have to pray that the car behind you doesn't smack into your vehicle whilst you are doing your thing.

Now that ends the digression on the digression. Back to my story.

Excuse me for another second. I just realized that I got some cream cheese on the keyboard of this typewriter. I am eating a bagel with a schmear of cream cheese, and I guess I am being a little

This was a bagel with a schmear, but as soon as we put the cream cheese on, the Gabby Cabby ate it. Sorry.

sloppy. Would you like to see what a bagel with a schmear of cream cheese looks like? So, take a look...

If you just hold tight, let me wipe the cream cheese off the keyboard and get back to typing my story.

AUTHOR PAUSES...

AUTHOR CLEANS KEYBOARD...

AUTHOR RESUMES HIS STORY...

It was about eleven in the morning in lower Manhattan, and I was waved over by a guy who I immediately knew to be a radio reporter for the British Broadcasting Corp., even before he got into my taxi. Just one look at my passenger standing on that street corner told me that his name was Douglas Campbell and that he was from the United Kingdom.

I just lied to you. I didn't have the slightest idea who the guy was until he told me. I just wanted to fool you a little into thinking I know all and see all. Where is it written that I can't pull your leg a little?

So Douglas introduces himself to me and tells me who he is and says, "Do you know how to get to Brooklyn Heights?" I respond the way a real live New York City taxi driver would respond. "What is this, a test? Are you working for the city? Do I look like someone who was milking Bessie in Iowa last week?"

If I had been in a bad mood, Douglas really would have been in trouble. As it was, I mumbled to myself about him, "Putz."

You see, dear reader, aren't you glad that I explained to you what a "putz" is. Now, you are in the "in" crowd.

Whilst we were crossing the Brooklyn Bridge—by the way, that is my second use of the word "whilst." I love that word, and you should keep track of the number of times that I use it in this book—Douglas said that he wanted to interview me for the BBC because "I was the typical New York City taxi driver."

Faster than you could say "shazam," I replied, "I am not the typical New York City taxi driver. I speak English."

Now I should like to point out to all of you politically correct types who happen to be reading these words, that if you think I was, by making that statement, making fun of Third World people who are driving taxis on the streets of New York City, you can bet your sweet ass, I was.

There are more than sixty thousand cabdrivers in the City of New York, and I honestly believe that there are only six who can speak English. There is myself and the five guys who used to work on Wall Street as brokers before they were downsized.

Douglas of BBC thought my line about speaking English was so funny. Big deal, this from a guy who lives in a country where they think Monty Python and Benny Hill are humor. If the truth be known, I think the British have terrible comedy, and their singing is nothing to shake a stick at.

How do I know this? Well, later in this book, I will tell you how some Brits flew me over to England so I could give a speech in a big castle. I had a great time because I got to see wenches. I had an even better time because I didn't pay for it.

Anyway, Douglas of BBC recorded my pontifications about life in the Big Apple.

He was like so many young folk who travel to New York City to find their fame and fortune. Only in his case he had traveled first to London to join with the British Broadcasting Corp. and then on to the Big Apple for broadcast material.

I never thought of myself as "broadcast material."

Our little cab ride was for two purposes it seems. Yes, Douglas did want some material, but at the same time he indicated that we were crossing over into Brooklyn so that he could see a girl that he knew.

Now, let us stop here for a minute and consult our financial experts in the readership. Am I not correct to assume that if Douglas was just going to see a girl in Brooklyn, that would be classified as merely a trip to possibly muffky fuffky and therefore not reimbursable or tax deductible?

On the other hand, if he were to interview a cabdriver on the way, wouldn't that make it possible for the cost of the little joyride to be placed on an entirely delightful line on the expense sheet?

Frankly, I had not thought about this at the time because I deal in cash, and I never get into the world of reimbursements and taxes. Poor Douglas, he made me what I am today, and I just got him into trouble.

Well, let that be a lesson to him. I hope it keeps him away from other English-speaking taxi drivers. I don't want the competition.

Douglas asked me about the daily duties of a cabdriver in New York City.

I told him that a cabdriver should have a good knowledge of the city. You should know how to get along with people. It doesn't hurt to know how to drive. But the most important thing, more than anything else as far as the Taxi and Limousine Commission was concerned, you have to have sixty dollars for the hack license.

I started to explain further to Douglas that when you go for the physical, a doctor, as part of the examination, holds a part of your anatomy and asks you to cough. That section of our interview ended up on the BBC cutting room floor.

A big mistake. I thought I was quite vivid in my description, and it could have served some educational purpose.

Frankly, I have never understood why doctors do that procedure. Is there some kind of a correlation between your crotch and your throat? Also, why do some doctors take so long when they do it?

As we crossed the Brooklyn Bridge, I pointed out to Douglas that it was fairly unusual for me to be driving to Brooklyn. Most cabdrivers like to stay in midtown Manhattan where the money is.

The other problem, I explained to him, was that I was probably going to come back empty since Brooklyn people don't take cabs to Manhattan, and if you are the driver doing it, you have to be lucky enough to find that passenger.

That, by the way, is the scam that you use to get a good tip out of a possible one-way trip. Tell the passenger your problem, and maybe, just maybe, if you are lucky, he will consider your empty ride back when figuring out the tip.

You see, Douglas was thinking about his girl and possible muffky fuffky. I was thinking about getting as much money out of this guy as I could. Was there anyone in the cab who was worried about the British Broadcasting Corp.? I think not.

But I did tell him some cute stories about my cab driving. If I remember correctly (like I don't have a gazillion copies of that broadcast all around my house) the best one was about the guy who shot his car on the Brooklyn Bridge.

A number of months before, a gentleman's vehicle just died in the middle of the bridge.

He got out and lifted the hood and started pulling and pushing all those little wires that nobody knows where they lead to. Nothing happened.

The cars that were now being blocked behind contained drivers who were not exactly thrilled about this abrupt change in their movement. There was no movement.

Beep! Beep! Beep! The Brooklyn Bridge was fast becoming a parking lot.

Not too tolerant, not too understanding of the problem this guy was having.

Beep! Beep! Beep!

Hurl invectives. Hurl more invectives. Use of a great many dirty words. A variety of finger gestures.

The driver finally cracked as his protagonists knew would happen. After all, these were my kind of drivers.

He pulled out a revolver and proceeded to shoot the car. Over and over until he ran out of bullets, he punctured the door, the hood, the trunk.

It was now really dead. Murder on the Brooklyn Bridge.

The cops showed up and took the guy into custody. Listen, you can do a great many weird things in this city, but come on, you just don't shoot your car.

That man, I told Douglas, had become a legend. And because of his exploits a new type of banter between drivers and pump jockeys now happened at gasoline stations all around the city.

Drivers would say,

"Fill it up with gasoline"

"Please check the oil"

"And, if you don't mind, reload my pistol."

I was on a roll with Douglas, so I figured I would hit him with another tale. If I could, maybe he would be so interested in what I was telling he might get mixed up as to the exchange rate between English pounds and U.S. dollars, and my day would be made.

I was hoping that I hit the mother lode with this bloke. (Isn't that what the Brits call themselves?)

Gee. Maybe I could make the bloke broke. I liked the sound of that phrase as I softly mumbled it to myself.

The next tale I told him was the one about the car that shot the driver. Only kidding.

I related to him my wonderful encounter with a guy who got into the taxi with a rottweiler and told me that the pet was sick and that he hoped "my dog doesn't throw up in the back of your cab." Just what every cabdriver wants to hear, right?

Traffic usually moves at about five miles an hour on the streets of Manhattan. I like to say that if I want to run someone over I have to get out of the cab to do it.

I took that guy from his house to the veterinarian's office at racetrack speed. I was a nervous wreck, and for once I was so intent on driving I didn't say a word.

Glad to report I made it, and the back of the hack remained clean. However, the next passenger gets into the cab and says, "You ought to smell the perfume I am smelling in the back of your cab. Some of these broads use stuff that makes them smell like a dog."

And a few weeks later my chat with Douglas Campbell was heard by 150 million people in fifty-one countries. Not bad for my first gig in the broadcasting business.

Are you getting into this story? Take a break. Go get something to eat, something to drink, come back to the book, I'll wait here.

PAUSE

PAUSE

Hello. You are back. I was worried that maybe you weren't enjoying this as much as I am. This is a dream come true. To talk to someone, and they can't even get in a word edgewise. Now that is my kind of taxi ride.

Where was I?

I don't remember, but before I do continue my tales I better tell you a little more about me.

Turn the page.

Have You Ever Seen a Bronx Bomber?

A long time ago in a galaxy far, far, away[3]...there was probably a place called "The Bronx."

You see, I am firmly convinced that The Bronx I grew up in, which is one of the five boroughs of New York City, could not have been created for only one place in the universe.

First a little geography. The other four boroughs of the city are Manhattan, Queens, Brooklyn, and Staten Island. Notice none of them has the word "The" in front of them. That is because once upon a time the entire area we now call "The Bronx" was actually owned by a family called the Broncks. People used to say, "We are going up to see the Broncks" much the way they would have said, "We are going to see the Smiths or the Joneses."

Each of the boroughs has a certain style.

Manhattan is where you have people who do not know how to boil water and who actually send out for instant coffee. It is the place where if you give a lady a ring less than

---

[3] *Star Wars*; George Lucas

one carat it is considered nothing more than a friendship ring. This is the only place in the world where you would find the following conversation between two people who live in one of the high-rise apartment buildings:

"I am growing corn this season."

"How tall is your corn?"

"My corn is eighteen stories tall."

This kind of a conversation would take place especially along Second or First avenues in the Fifties, the Sixties, the Seventies (I am referring to streets, not years), which I would call the groovy eastside.

I would call the people living in this area rich. Not very rich and certainly not filthy rich. But the common thread of almost everyone living in this area is that they live in the somewhat fast lane.

They go to Boca Raton, Florida, the Hamptons, Long Island, New York, Aspen, Colorado, and places like that for vacations. Their only connection to taxicabs and their drivers is that they use them to go to the airport.

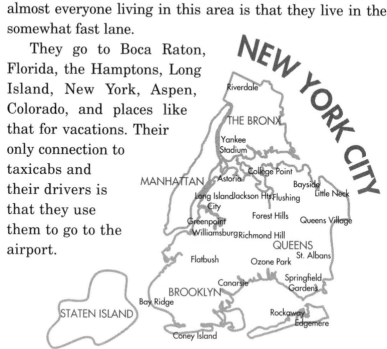

The buildings, which are guarded by doormen, have terraces. And let me tell you about those terraces.

How would you like to stand on something that is forty stories up and about five long by five wide? I don't remember ever hearing of a terrace falling in the street, but I can tell you when I get on one, I stand with my back to the wall of the building, and I don't look down.

Yes, I know that I am making generalizations here, but this is really a good description of that area, and anyway, this is my book and I will say what I want.

If you have read to this point, it is too late for you to get your money back.

And don't think I can be intimidated because you bought the book in the first place. Big deal. You have any idea of what I get for each book? I do better fishing coins out of pay phones on the streets of Manhattan.

Come to think of it, I shall tell you about that a little later.

Here is the real point. Manhattan is made up of many sections. Some of them you have heard of, like Greenwich Village, Chinatown, Little Italy, Times Square. Each has a distinct flavor and composition of people.

I love to tell people when I am showing them Manhattan that there actually is only one group of people who all work for me, and what they do is run to the next section before I get there, change clothing, and act in a new way.

"Attention all personnel. I am bringing tourists next to Black Harlem. Please be singing gospel songs and mumbling 'Lordie, Lordie,' by the time we get there. Then be prepared to move on to Little Italy where you will act like you're in a scene from *The Godfather*."

1 White Hall
2 Wall Street
3 Tribeca
4 Lower Broadway
5 Chinatown
6 Lower East Side
7 SOHO
8 Little Italy
9 Bowery
10 Greenwich Village
11 East Village
12 Chelsea
13 Grammercy
14 Stuyvesant
15 Garment District
16 Murray Hill
17 Tudor City
18 Lower West Side
19 Theatre District
20 Midtown
21 Lincoln Center Area
22 Upper East Side
23 Upper West Side
24 Central Park
25 Yorkville
26 Morningside Heights
27 Harlem
28 East Harlem

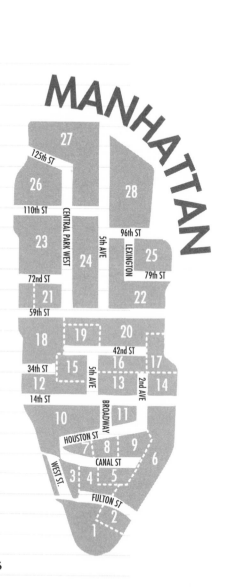

I have often wondered, by the way, which came first, the Mafia or Hollywood's impression of the Mafia?

That is exactly what Manhattan is. A whole bunch of very different neighborhoods with some very different people. That "melting pot" that you have heard so much about hasn't really happened. It is like the ingredients in a stew which has yet to be cooked.

When I was a kid growing up in The Bronx, it was real neat to take the subway down to Madison Square Garden, which at that time was in Manhattan at Fiftieth Street and Eighth Avenue.

Now it has been rebuilt at Thirty-third and Seventh Avenue in Manhattan, and it kind of covers the Pennsylvania Railroad Station. By the by, it isn't square. It happens to be round. It is named "Square" because the original one was at a place called Madison Square.

Even as kids we realized that the people living downtown were different from us.

Of course that didn't stop us from being boisterous and obnoxious. As a matter of fact, I remember once being part of a group that threw Cracker Jacks on the basketball court during a game at the Garden.

I just had to get that episode in my book. And there, I have done it.

Don't you just marvel at all the writers who tell it as it was. They talk of their affairs, their crimes, their wicked deeds.

Now that I have put those few lines in my book, the publisher can advertise this book as telling all.

"Gabby Cabby Reveals Cracker Jack Incident!"

"What really happened at the Garden?"

"He really did have sticky fingers!"

"This book is a must-read basketball adventure!"

Well, I hope you get a chance to visit Manhattan and take me to lunch.

It seems as if almost everyone in the world has visited New York City, but they just haven't been taking me out to lunch. What I am trying to do now is start the trend of "Buy The Gabby Cabby A Meal Program."

A piece of trivia for you—New York City is the number-one tourist attraction in the world.

And remember, if you need a cab, look for me. I am in the yellow one.

Enough with Manhattan. Let us move on to Queens.

Well, that's it for Queens, let us move on to Brooklyn.

Hold it. That was sort of mean to the fine folks who live in Queens. Their problem is that Manhattan people who don't live in Queens consider it merely a bedroom community. A place to sleep but not a place to "live."

The foolish folks in Manhattan look down on Queens. It is really very nice. When the tennis season rolls around, and all of society shows up at the big matches which are held in that borough at places like Forest Hills, then people in Manhattan will fight to get into Queens.

That reminds me, Queens has a number of New York's very large cemeteries so people do really die to get into that borough for things other than tennis.

Actually, the filled cemeteries have given birth to a generation of liars. You are invited to the church or synagogue to say farewell to the dearly departed. That's fine. You go, but you certainly don't want to sit in a car for two hours to go out to a cemetery in the suburbs because the ones in the city are all filled.

So you lie. You say that you have an important meeting with the prime minister of Nepal, and you just can't go out to the suburban cemetery. The problem is that everyone else is also making up a lie, so yours better be pretty convincing. Like I said, a generation of liars because the city's cemeteries are full.

The borough of Staten Island is someplace over there. I and all other cabdrivers know very little about this mysterious island because it is on the other side of our harbor and you drive there by either a bridge, which costs a bunch of dollars, or a ferryboat that takes twenty minutes.

If you think a New York City taxi driver is going to spend time on a ferry or time fighting with a passenger as to who should pay the toll, then you must really be having something stronger than tea in your cup.

In almost every movie Hollywood has made about the cops in New York City, there is absolutely, positively some big shot criminal who threatens to have the officer who is interrogating him sent to a police precinct in Staten Island.

Can you imagine the cross that the fine people of Staten Island have had to bear because of that image? Well, tough potatoes to them.

Do you catch my drift? Do I have to spell it out to you? It isn't where the action is.

Brooklyn, on the other hand, is a very special place. We Bronx guys loved to date Brooklyn girls. They all wore tight skirts, lots of makeup, and very high heels. They all lived in houses. We were living in apartment buildings.

People in Brooklyn have finished basements with very impressive bars, and they put plastic on their living room furniture, which makes your bottom hot in the summer and cold in the winter. One other thing, Brooklyn girls were great kissers. I think it was the abundance of lipstick that made them taste so good.

If it wasn't a part of New York City, Brooklyn would be the fourth largest city in the United States. If you ask a Brooklyn person where they come from, they will not say New York City.

So, I have given you a rough picture of the four unimportant boroughs of the City of New York. Now let us take a look at the one I grew up in.

But, be it ever so humble, there was no place like home, and for me home was The Bronx.

It was there that I decided I wanted to grow up to be a U-boat commander in the German navy. Ach! let me explain, mein readers.

There was a park that was directly opposite my apartment building, and in it there was a rock formation that looked to me like it was a U-boat. Keep in mind that a great many movies were made after World War II about those ships.

The U-boat commander was a bastard, of course, who sank the helpless ships on the surface. But he was the driver. He commanded his vehicle. He abused other transportation.

I don't remember when it happened, but at some point I decided that if I couldn't be a U-boat commander, at least I could have the characteristics by driving a cab on the streets of New York City.

Maybe that is why I love to yell "schwine, pig dog" at a cabdriver who dares to cut me off for a fare.

When I was living in The Bronx, my neighborhood, which was right near the Yankee Stadium, had three definite groups. Two were in residence and one was transient. Now, let us see if you can figure out who lived there and who just worked there of the following three groups:

Jewish People

Catholic People

Black People (now referred to as African Americans)

As a hint to you, one of the three above groups contained the maids who came to clean.

Bingo, if you guessed that the Blacks were the maids, you guessed right.

As I remember it, every Jewish family had a maid who came to clean at least once a week, and she was referred to as "the girl" (even if she was eighty years old). She would work for the family for years and years and always end up being present at all bar mitzvahs and weddings.

I remember quite clearly at one of these occasions overhearing the only nonwhite, "the girl," in the temple dance hall, mumbling the following words to herself:

"Lord, please Lord, send these people some rhythm."

By the way, I just realized that a few paragraphs ago I mentioned that my neighborhood was right near Yankee

Yankee Stadium

Stadium. The thought occurs to me that there might be one reader in the world who doesn't know what that place is.

Well, it is the most famous baseball park in the United States, and it is where people like Babe Ruth, Joe DiMaggio, and Lou Gehrig played. Growing up near it was real neat.

The Bronx was a great place to learn about thoughtfulness and caring.

I remember the day—when I was a student in the third grade at Public School 35—the principal walked into our class and said, "Mrs. Hooper, your teacher, will not be in today. She was hit by a bus."

The entire class cheered.

It was also the place where you could learn the true meaning of love. I was madly in love with a girl named Barbara Gibgot in the seventh grade, and I thought about her day and night.

Perhaps that is why, whenever I saw her, I called her "vomit face."

I had my first date in The Bronx at a place called the Loew's Paradise, a famous movie theater (at that time). I don't remember the girl's name. Tragically, it was not Barbara Gibgot.

Did you know that a human arm can actually go from its socket in the shoulder around the back of a movie theater seat and then reach a breast?

Two other things I learned well in The Bronx. One was the art of deceit.

When my father thought he smelled smoke on my clothes, I told him I had been burning trash in a vacant lot. I certainly wasn't smoking cigarettes, sir.

A "vacant lot" was a very important thing to us kids. It was a place where a building had once been. The building was torn down, and now we were all just waiting for a new building to be built on that spot.

It was our ball field, our picnic area, our hidden treasure island. My favorite lot was the one at One Hundred Sixty-third Street and the Grand Concourse. I will always hate the people who eventually built 930 Grand Concourse on that corner.

The other thing I learned to do in The Bronx was drive a motor vehicle.

Hmmm. The art of deceit (telling a lie about smoking to my dad) and how to drive. The perfect foundation for being a New York City taxi driver.

Time to move on. Enough with the memories.

Ooops. I almost forgot to tell you what a Bronx Bomber is. That is what we people call a New York Yankee baseball slugger.

Put the Bags in the Trunk Yourself, Your Arm Isn't Broken

A re you talking to me? Are you talking to me? Are you talking to me?[4] Thanks a lot, Robert DeNiro. In one wonderful movie called *Taxi Driver*, you were able to set the occupation of being a taxi driver to a different level.

Instead of being considered the low man on the totem pole of vocations, I was now able to be considered pure garbage. A wacko. Deranged.

But I got to tell you, when that movie came out I figured, "If you can't stand the heat, get out of the kitchen"—or should I say, the cab?

Anyway, who cares what people might think? I think that the most fun job on the face of the Earth is being a cab-driver on the streets of New York.

When I first started, many of the drivers actually owned their own taxis.

---

[4]*Taxi Driver*; Paul Schrader, writer; Martin Scorcese, producer of the film

I can remember going out with a girl in The Bronx whose father was the owner and the driver of a cab. They were real people. A daddy, a mommy, a couple of sisters, and a brother.

They lived over in the east part of the borough where the working people lived. I guess it would be nice to say that I admired the girl's father very much. It was he who inspired me to become a cabdriver. I shall use that bit in my movie, come to think of it.

Picture the scene. The young man has come to take the girl to the dance. Dad the cabdriver is there to greet and check out the suitor.

"Son, with your brains and your talents you could be a doctor, an engineer, an architect, but if you really want to go someplace in this world, be a cabdriver and drive on the streets of New York City for twelve hours every day."

The girl's father (do you notice how I just can't remember her name like I did in the case of Barbara Gibgot?) didn't give me that speech, but he did say something about bringing his daughter home a virgin like he was sending her out.

Excuse me. Are you talking to me? Are you talking to me? If that girl was a virgin before we dated, then it is time to adjust all our maps so that they indicate that the world is flat.

Whether or not she was a woman of the world, as I suspected, this was something I was not about to find out about any woman until a number of years later. I was under the impression that if you had sex with a girl you had to marry her, and I just didn't want to get married that week.

You see, sex in The Bronx was much simpler in those days.

Have sex.

Find out about the baby coming.

Get married.

Now what did it mean to own a cab in those days?

It meant that the owner-driver could keep all of the money from the passengers minus the cost of buying the cab, the cost of paying for the medallion (which gave you the right to have a cab), the maintenance on the cab, the insurance on the cab, the taxes, and a bunch of other stuff.

This all meant that if you pulled in two thousand dollars a month, you ended up with about thirty cents net. Only kidding, you made a living.

Speaking of "making a living," that reminds me of the story about the pedestrian who was run down by a cab. The taxi driver rushed to the injured man's side and put his jacket under the man's head. "Are you comfortable?" the taxi driver asked him. The man responded, "I make a living."

Let me tell you, I know there is some literary critic type out there who just gasped because I interrupted my story to tell a joke. This is probably illegal in the writing world. Well, too bad. I am the driver of this book, and I drive it my way.

The problem, of course, is how to get back to my story now that I interrupted myself. I know. I shall make an illegal U-turn.

The owner of the cab would be on the road for twelve hours each day. What does he do about the other twelve hours in a day? If he was smart, he would have a driver who worked for him. The driver would get about half the proceeds of his shift. The other half would be kept by the owner.

This was a wonderful system because it encouraged the owners to have the best possible drivers working for them.

Not to worry. You just know that if something is working fine it should be screwed up by a bunch of politicians and bureaucrats.

The game plan was abruptly changed a number of years ago so that now a driver pays the owner about one hundred dollars for a twelve-hour shift. Everything he makes after that one hundred is the driver's to keep.

The reason the new system has hurt the taxi industry in

New York City is that there is now a tendency for owners not to care who is driving for them. As long as they get the hundred bucks, it isn't their problem.

Maybe now you kind of realize why the requirement to be a New York City taxi driver is the ability to breathe and have a hundred dollars.

"Driver, please take me to the Statue of Liberty."

"What's that?"

Since I am not a social scientist or an economic planner, the problems of the taxi industry are not mine. I do OK, and I love the work.

Wouldn't you want a job where you get to hear other people's most confidential conversations? Wouldn't you want a job where you get to meet a new person every five minutes who has a new destination for you?

Gadzooks! I love it so. Let me give you an example.

I pick up these two old broads on Park Avenue. Excuse me, I mean elderly ladies.

They are going to La Guardia Airport to catch a flight for their vacation spot. I guarantee you, they were in their seventies.

As we are hurtling on the Grand Central Parkway toward the airport, the two of them are discussing how they are going to pick up men. I am getting to hear in great detail what they intend to do to with these men.

Naturally, some of this really surprises me because I always thought that old people have brittle bones and should not put themselves in positions which will make them look like pretzels.

Frankly, the thought occurred to me that maybe I should

stop and buy them some calcium pills.

Anyway, by the time we get to the airport I am blushing like a teenager on his first date. I mean, after all, I was hearing language that would make a sailor blush.

And furthermore, I thought at a couple of places I was going to careen off the road.

Can you imagine the police report. Two old broads and a driver with a smile on his face found dead in a New York City cab? Let them figure that one out.

When we arrived at the airport, I wondered was I supposed to pay them, maybe?

I went back to the garage and took a cold shower.

Hold it. Don't go away. I have another example for you.

An elderly gentleman gets into my taxi at Roosevelt Hospital and gives me an address at which I presume he is staying.

I know what you are thinking. Doesn't this guy ever pick up young people? Sure, I do. I will tell you about them in the young people's chapter later on. My publisher told me that if I can appeal to the elderly, I am sure to get a best-seller out of this.

Anyway, on the way to the destination with the elderly gentleman, he is very quiet.

Very quiet.

Very, very quiet.

Very, very, very quiet.

He is dead.

That is why he is quiet.

What to do? Shall I just go through his pockets and drop him in the East River? Not a good idea. That is probably a sin. I am sure it is against some law.

So I drive to the nearest police station to report that I have a stiff in the backseat of my cab. The desk officer tells me there will be a twenty-minute wait.

I am thinking that maybe I came in the busy season. Maybe there are other cabdrivers in front of me who also have a dead body in the back of their cab.

Was I going to have to take a number like I was in a bakery?

Finally, I got waited on. An officer came out to the cab to survey the situation. Just like Sherlock Holmes, he was. The man was blue. The man wasn't breathing. The man was dead. Elementary, my dear taxi driver.

The police officer asked me if I had murdered the passenger. I assured him that I would never ever kill a passenger until the fare was paid, and, as he could see on the taxi meter, I had not yet been paid.

I then had to fill out form after form.

It all started to come together on the last form where I was asked the question, "How did you know that the passenger was dead?"

I filled in—"He wasn't laughing at my jokes."

If you were paying attention a few paragraphs back, I said something about going for a cold shower at the taxi garage. I can assure you that sentence was only put there to get a laugh from you. Did you laugh? My garage certainly doesn't have a shower of any kind.

The garage I work out of, and have for a number of years, is fairly typical of the taxi establishments in New York City.

First of all, it is not a garage. It is a parking lot. It is a lot that has no running water, and the bathroom facilities are two portable toilets. The only place where you can be either warm in the winter or cool in the summer is in the trailer office where they collect the money for your shift.

It is not a very nice place, and, frankly, most of the taxi companies in the Big Apple have facilities just exactly like that.

But before you get upset about my working conditions and how mean my taxi owner must be, let me point out to you that if you really want to see a crap house, come with me to the Central Taxi Hold facilities at either of our two airports, La Guardia and the John F. Kennedy International Airport.

Once you take a passenger to the airport, you have the option to either come back into Manhattan empty or go to Central Taxi Hold and wait in a long line to be called to one of the terminals. If you really want to be a student of terrible bathroom facilities that will turn your stomach, they are the places to go.

Central Taxi Hold is a relatively new concept run by the Port Authority, which runs the airports. The Port Authority is administered by an executive board jointly appointed by the governors of the states of New York and New Jersey.

These are the folks who own the harbor, the bridges, the tunnels, the airports, and the World Trade Center. So much money is pulled in from things like the George Washington Bridge tolls that they are certainly the richest such organization on the planet.

By the way, the George Washington Bridge, the Holland Tunnel, and the Lincoln Tunnel were built back in the 1930s and were only supposed to have tolls until the tunnels were paid for. Fifty years later and they still haven't been "paid for."

If those fat cats don't care about my toilet needs, why should my taxi owner invest in something nice for me?

I know what you are now thinking. Enough with the bathroom talk, let us get some more cab action here.

Well, just one more toilet story.

For years I have been aware of the fact that although we have two portable toilets at our lot, one is always locked.

I was under the impression that it was just broken and that someday the honey dipper would come and drain it and fix it. (A honey dipper is a country expression for the guy who takes care of the cesspool, and I am now showing off to you that I am a man of much knowledge.)

Recently I noticed the dispatcher, while no one was looking except me, take a key out of his pocket and use it to go into the presumably nonworking toilet.

After what I thought was a fairly lengthy stay, he exited, locked the door, and went back to his office.

Unbelievable. I realized that I was looking at the Executive Casa Commode Grande. There was one toilet for the drivers and one for the masters. Theirs was never broken. We drivers were being discriminated against.

Look, everything is a state of mind. It is not the problems of life. It is how you deal with them. I took that incident and have turned it into a positive thing for me.

I have a dream.

A dream to someday get a key to that wondrous place and be able to use it. Yes, my friends, a dream in which I, the maestro of the city's streets, will be able to know the pleasure of being one of the "in" crowd.

I think I have time for one more taxi story before this chapter ends, and here it is.

If you want to make good money driving a cab in the Big Apple, you have to know where to go for passengers.

For instance, hookers are wonderful rides, and it is great to take them home.

You filthy little reader. I don't mean I ride the hookers, and I don't mean I take them to my home. I am trying to say that they are good passengers, and I like to take them to their home merely as a destination.

They tell wonderful stories of what they have done during the evening just past, and that is why I love to go to those spots where I know they wait for a cab to go home.

If you want a list of those spots, please send a self-addressed envelope along with ten thousand dollars to the publisher of this book.

By the way, hookers never ever proposition a cabdriver in lieu of the fare. The only people who seem to do that are people who claim they are gypsies.

"Would you like me to read your palm so you know your future, my handsome driver?"

"I don't think so."

"But, my gorgeous, smart driver, I would be pleased to read your palm, and you would then be pleased not to charge me for the trip."

"Listen, lady, the only thing you are going to read at the end of this trip is the meter."

Anyway, one night two hookers get in the cab at the corner of Fifty-seventh Street and Seventh Avenue. (Well, I had to tell you one of the good places because you did spend your hard-earned money for this book.)

That is right. The ladies of the night hang out where Carnegie Hall is located. You know the old line, "How do you get to Carnegie Hall?"

Practice. Practice. Practice.

I can tell you the two hookers that night didn't need to practice. They were accomplished professionals.

Stop the book. I will not go on with my story until I get a chance to tell you a very funny joke about a hooker.

This guy wants to have a real hot time, and he goes to Laverne's House of Pleasure and tells the madam that he wants something real kinky. The madam suggests Hurricane Gussie.

Just that name, Hurricane Gussie, indicates to our man that he is in for a good time, and his palms start to sweat, and his heart starts to pound.

He walks his way up to Hurricane Gussie's room, and no sooner does he sit down on her bed, she throws water in his face.

"What is that for?" he asks.

"That is the rain," she responds.

Our man is feeling good. He feels that he is in for some real kinky muffky fuffky.

Then she puts on a big fan in the room, and it starts blowing in his face.

"What is that for?" he asks.

"That is the wind," she responds.

All of sudden, Hurricane Gussie starts pounding on the metal part of the bed with a hammer.

"What is that for?" he asks.

"That is the thunder," she responds.

Hurricane Gussie announces that she is now ready for action.

But our man gets up and starts to walk out of the room.

"Wait a minute. Where do you think you are going?" she asks.

"I can't perform in weather like this," he responds.

And now, back to my real hooker story.

All the way out to Queens where they live, the two hookers are talking about a guy they took care of during the evening. They are telling me about the fact that he wanted them to sing while they were fooling around.

"Sing? Sing? Sing what?" I asked.

They told me that he wanted them to sing the "Star-Spangled Banner" as they did you know what. Of course, being business professionals, they sang.

The point of this story is how some things can influence your thoughts later in life. Ever since that trip, whenever I hear the "Star-Spangled Banner" played, I stand just a little taller.

And just think. Every time you hear the "Star-Spangled Banner," from this point on, you will think of those two hookers singing it to some guy in New York City.

And, if the guy next to you is smiling, you will know he also bought this book.

I Say, Old Chap, We Would Like to Hear You on This Side of the Pond

W han that April with his showres soote, the drought of March hath perced to the roote, and bathed every vein in swich licour, of which vertu engendred is the flowr...[5]

Born in London, son of John and Agnes Chaucer, Geoffrey was probably the most famous taxi driver of all time. When he wasn't tooling around in his yellow cab, he would, from time to time, write a thing or two.

And, if you don't believe me about good old Geoffrey Chaucer, then you are just as bad as all the other people who think New York City taxi drivers cannot be trusted to tell the truth. Big deal, so occasionally we take you past the same statue nine times. Does that mean we are not deserving of your faith and trust?

I am thinking of London now. Remember that Brit who got into my cab earlier in this book? He interviewed me, took the tape back to England, did some fancy editing, and lo and behold it was aired on something called the BBC World Service.

---

[5]Geoffrey Chaucer; *The Canterbury Tales*; Signet Classics

35

Now let me explain something to those who think guys like Don Imus, Howard Stern, Rush Limbaugh, and Paul Harvey are big deals with big number radio audiences. The number of people who listen to them collectively doesn't even come close to the number who heard me on that fateful day.

Are you ready for the total? Hold your breath. Sit down. Here it comes.

More than one hundred fifty million people in fifty-one countries heard my voice. You want to talk big. Talk about the BBC World Service.

But I didn't know that at the time. I knew it was going to be aired, but I figured my interview would probably be heard by three people in Altoona, Pennsylvania.

About a week after I was on the airwaves, I got a telephone call from a guy named Douglas Cameron. (Don't get mixed up here. The guy who interviewed me in the cab was Douglas Campbell. I guess English parents like to name their kids "Douglas.")

Douglas Cameron was and, as of the writing of this book, is a big deal presenter on a station that was called LBC. It is in London. It was the first commercial station (privately owned) in the United Kingdom. Today, it is called LNT, and it is still cooking up a storm for its listeners.

He told me that he had heard me on the BBC broadcast and would like to start telephoning me once a week to get the news about New York City. He explained that people were fascinated with the Big Apple, and he thought I had a pretty neat style.

The word "neat" is mine. Douglas Cameron does not say "neat."

Hey! I thought it would be great to schmooze with this guy. Isn't that what cabdrivers do? Talk. And talk. And then talk some more.

Just as we were to end the call, he said, "Oh, by the way, we will send you thirty pounds every time we call you." I said sure, but I really didn't understand what he was talking about.

Honestly, that part about the thirty pounds kind of flew past me, and I really didn't think about it until I got another telephone call about a week later from a gentleman named Pat Kenny, who is the big man at RTE, which is the main radio network in the Republic of Ireland. Pat was calling from Dublin.

He said that he had heard me on the BBC and thought it would be great fun to call me a couple of times a month, and I would give a report about New York City. He explained that people were fascinated with the Big Apple, and he thought that I had a pretty neat style.

The word "neat" is mine. Pat Kenny does not say "neat."

Of course I agreed. What could be better than one radio station telephoning a New York City cabdriver? Two radio stations calling a New York City cabdriver.

You can see it coming can't you. As Pat was saying goodbye, he said that his station would send me forty U.S. dollars every time we talked.

Listen carefully, kids, my mother didn't raise any stupid children. I looked at my wife, she looked at me, and we both realized that we had really stepped into something.

Here is what we did.

We got the fax address, and if that didn't exist, the mailing address for almost every radio station in the English-speaking world. I am talking about the United States, Canada, South Africa, Australia, New Zealand, Hong Kong, Scotland, Northern Ireland, Wales, Singapore.

And here is what we sent them:

Dear Boss:

I am a New York City taxi driver who is in an ideal situation to give your listeners the most fun reports about this wonderful city of mine.

I can give you a telephone number that I will answer 24 hours a day, 7 days a week, 365 days a year.

Sometimes I will be answering your call in my house, sometimes it will be in the garage, sometimes it will be in the cab, and who knows, maybe sometimes in the shower.

Here are some of the typical stories I will have for you, and I want to assure you that they are True Tales. I don't have to make up anything.

The man who shot his car on the Brooklyn Bridge.

The showgirl who took her clothes off in the back of my taxi.

The passenger who died in my cab.

I will also be telling your nice listeners of the famous people who I see on the street and the ones who ride with me.

I look forward to hearing from you.

Very truly yours,

Peter Franklin

Holy Talk Radio! We were off and running. I started getting calls and faxes from all over. I was in business, baby.

I quickly learned that although many of the presenters certainly wanted to have me on their shows, they never really knew exactly what to ask me, so my wife and I decided to move on to the next plateau.

We would type up a list of stories, call it True Tales, and fax it to the stations that had "booked" me for the coming week. They were stories about things happening in the city, things happening in the cab, and the reaction of the passengers to events that were occurring around the world.

For instance, I would have a story about thousands of people tap dancing in front of a major department store; a couple fighting in the cab about who forgot to bring the turkey for the party; street reaction to a scandal in some royal family.

That fax was just cut and paste at that time. Thank goodness for scissors and paste. But eventually we moved on to a computer to do the layout and transmission.

Each week our teenage son Nicholas would make a wonderful fax letter (now it is also sent out as an E-mail letter) that would go out to all the stations. This quickly became a piece of literature the stations looked forward to getting.

This preparation made life easier for the radio stations, and it made it easier for me to be prepared and do a better show.

A word of advice to you corporate moguls who are thinking of moving on to computers in your business. Go find a teenage kid.

Here I am. The Wacky Hacky, the Gabby Cabby, the Last English Speaking Cabdriver in New York. I am radio-active.
Spend a couple of moments with me on the telephone.
You and your listeners will enjoy my TRUE TALES™ from the streets of New York.

PETER

THE CABDRIVER

DO YOU REMEMBER THE GOOD OLD DAYS WHEN FOLKS WENT FISHING JUST FOR FISH? Some of the crooks in The Big Apple are now fishing for something else. Your bank deposit.

THE PHONE MAN YOU SEE MAY BE A WRONG NUMBER. Just when I figure all the scams have been tried here in New York City, the bad people dream up another one. When one of these phone repairers show up, you better hang on to your gotchkis or they might take that also.

IT IS BACK TO SCHOOL TIME AND THIS PARTICULAR PRODUCT FOR THE KIDDIES AIN'T FUNNY. The outside of the box has a picture of a nurse on it. Inside is a thing that nurses do use, but school children shouldn't, even if this one is a bit of a fake.

A NEW USE FOR THE AUTOMATED TELLER MACHINE IS ON ITS WAY. This story has something to do with punishing bad people, but it is something that will not make you law abiding citizens happy at all.

THE JOKE DU JOUR

REMEMBER...
I GIVE
TOURS!

CALL ME a TAXI!

EMAIL: nyctaxi@mcimail.com

SEND ME YOUR EMAIL ADDRESS!

http://gabby.com

Faxletter for the week of September 17

So week after week, month after month, year after year, the True Tales found its way into most radio stations throughout the world. And, because of that, I was able to create what I think is the most unique list in the world.

I have the name, the station, the E-mail address, and the fax address of just about every single radio personality in the world. I could, if I wanted to, contact every broadcasting entity within a matter of minutes.

Now, let us see, what would I write? I know. I would ask them to ask their listeners to each send me one dollar. Silly. Wouldn't work you say?

Oh yes it would because it was done once by accident.

I was talking to a talk show host in Rochester, New York. His broadcast name is Brother Weeze. American broadcasters have this thing about using stage names. It is something that is not done overseas.

Now Brother Weeze is well known not only to his audience but also to most other talk show hosts in the United States because—now how can I put this politely—HE IS MISSING A SCREW.

At some place in our conversation, I said, "People of Rochester, send me a dollar." I don't even remember why it came about. It was just one of those lines that fly out of our mouths, and afterward we wonder, "Why did I say that?"

Since I do have a flair for the dramatic, I shall end the story right now.

Thank-you and good-bye.

Wait a minute. I just got a call from my accountant. His firm is Dewey, Cheatum, and Howe. He says he wants me to continue the story so that he can find out whether or not those dollars came rolling in. Well OK, but I hope no one from the tax department is reading this book.

You bet your sweet bippy the dollars rolled in. It was actually quite terrifying to think that all you had to do was to ask nicely, and you would get money sent to you.

The total—are you ready—was about two hundred and twenty-five dollars. The moral of this story is that if you are ever down on your luck and need some money, just ask someone who listens to Brother Weeze in Rochester, New York.

I was concerned that I had broken some radio broadcasting rule of the Federal Communications Act, and I considered immediately leaving for the jungle in some Third World country.

After all, I don't think you are supposed to mooch money from radio audiences. Unless, of course, you are a sponsor.

Which brings up my next subject. Are you aware of the fact that in some places in the world the radio stations are commercial operations, and in others they are noncommercial and just a voice of the government involved?

For instance, the British Broadcasting Corp. doesn't accept advertising, but it is pretty free to broadcast almost everything. There have been instances, however, where the government "influences" its broadcasting.

For instance, for many years, the voice of Jerry Adams, the guy from the Irish Republican Army in Northern Ireland, was never permitted to be heard on any of the BBC programs.

In Singapore (they love me in Singapore), the station is certainly subjected to government control. You have to be careful what you say on their airwaves.

During the period when the world was talking about the flogging of some American kid who spray-painted cars on a street in Singapore, I was advised that any flogging jokes would not be appreciated.

That didn't stop me from doing it every other place in the world. I had a little tape player which gave out the sound of a whip. The presenter, upon hearing the noise, would, of course, ask "What's that?"

I responded that it was the whip I used to flog passengers in my cab—a new service that was just fifty cents. I added that luckily for me, there were many people in New York City who really wanted to be flogged in the back of a taxi.

When I started broadcasting in South Africa on the South African Broadcasting Company, the national radio station, they used to tape me and then air it later because they were concerned that I might say something too controversial for their audience.

The taping gave them the opportunity to delete anything they didn't like. Keep in mind that for a long period of time, I was the only American being heard on South African radio because of the various boycotts over the apartheid policy.

Frankly, if it wasn't for a South African broadcaster named Patricia Glynn, the people of that country never would have gotten to hear me. She was the first broadcaster in the country with whom I did broadcasts, and I think to some extent she was putting her career on the line.

I should like to think that members of the hard-nosed ruling party at that time, upon hearing me on the air, realized that it was time to change their ways and bring freedom and equality to all its citizens.

Yes, and I also take responsibility for the invention of the wheel.

I have just realized that maybe I violated some Federal Communications Act regulation by broadcasting to South Africa at that time. Now I am really in big trouble. Oh well, I can always go hide in Brother Weeze's house.

As of the day I am writing this, I have done more than nine thousand "live" radio broadcasts for stations all over the world. I have kept very exact records of every single broadcast made, and I have at least one audiotape from almost every station that I have been on.

You got Zulus in South Africa, rubber tappers in Sri Lanka, ship captains in the China Sea, sheepherders in New Zealand, and many more folks who know of the Gabby Cabby.

Sure it was a golden opportunity, but my wife and I were smart enough to seize it and take it to new heights. I made sure, as I said, to always tell the truth. If I ever got caught in a broadcast lie, my credibility would be lost.

I have also made sure not to miss a broadcast. I can even remember a time when I was talking to Guy Phillips of KYKY in St. Louis, Missouri, and in between sentences, I was barfing because I was deathly ill. Now Guy will know why I was hesitating between sentences that day.

Today, we are modern. Thanks to our son Nicholas, our operation has become really high tech. We maintain a Web site which is http://gabby.com, and it is one of the most heavily accessed sites on the web because my broadcasters tell their listeners to look at it.

Let me be a bragging father. Nicholas's site was awarded the distinction of being rated in the top 5 percent by Point Communications, who awards such things.

My broadcast week runs from Sunday through Saturday. Each Saturday evening after the last show of the previous week, I have a meeting with my "staff." We discuss the stories for the coming week and the jokes that I will be telling.

The "staff" consists of Nicholas, his sister Catharine, and his brother Alexi, also teenagers.

This all reminds me of the story (you didn't really think I would make it through a chapter without telling a joke, did you?)...

It was at a service in a religious institution, and it came the time when the congregation was supposed to get up and make a statement of some religious significance.

"My name is Jacob, and I own the world's largest supermarket chain. But when I am in this holy building, I am nothing."

"My name is Arthur, and I am the principal shareholder in the world's largest airline, but when I am in this holy building, I am nothing."

"My name is Daniel, and I am the highest-paid actor in the world, but when I am in this holy building, I am nothing."

And after countless other very distinguished people made similar statements, first about their wealth and then the line about, "I am nothing," finally one man, a rather shabbily dressed man, stood up and said,

"My name is Richard, and I have no money, and I really have no successes to report, but I must tell you when I am in this holy building, I too am nothing."

To which one of the more prestigious people present shouted,

"Look who is trying to be a nothing."

Well, that is a wrap for this chapter, but I want you to keep this in mind. If you work hard at something you can be a success, but if that fails it is always possible to be a "nothing."

"Nothing" ain't so bad.

Go West, Young Man, Go West

Thishis field, this game, is a part of our past. It reminds us of all that was good and that could be good again. Oh, people will come, Ray. People will most definitely come.[6]

What I am talking about here is the "Field of Dreams," which is an actual baseball field in the middle of a cornfield in Iowa.

As you may remember, Kevin Costner made the movie, and the story was about a farmer who had this ball field, and to it came baseball players who were dead.

It is a poignant, lovely movie, and it touches each member of an audience in a different way.

The method by which the dead players appear and disappear is by way of the cornfield which surrounds the outfield. They come walking out of the cornfield, and after playing ball for awhile, they return to it.

Soon I will tell you the reason I came to be at that field, but first let me tell you about the field. And don't you dare

---

[6]Field Of Dreams; W.P. Kinsella; Phil Robinson, film director

skip and read ahead. I am running this book, and you are to play by my rules or I shall make you go to your room, and you will not be allowed to buy my next book.

When you arrive at the Field of Dreams, you just start playing baseball on the field with whoever happens to be playing already. Just the way you play a game in a New York City park, so I was already used to the deal.

I am proud to report that during my first time at bat, I smacked a line drive over the head of the shortstop. The ball continued through the legs of the left fielder and went into the cornfield behind.

Not bad for a New York City hacky. My next two times at bat were somewhat less spectacular, and, frankly, I won't tell you what I did.

I struck out twice. So I can't keep a secret. Big deal.

Once the game ended, I went over to the spot in the cornfield where I thought my first hit went. Good manners dictated that I should go and find that ball.

As I walked around looking for the baseball, I suddenly realized that I was deep enough so that I could no longer see the baseball field.

I found myself with the very strange feeling that the people and pets that I had loved, who were now gone, just might be in the field with me.

I must tell you that those few moments were some of the most delicious minutes I have ever had in my life. Just think how wonderful it is, if for just a short time you can see what you missed so much.

Wouldn't it be a tickle to tell your father what happened in the last ten years? How about letting your father-in-law know that you are still satisfied with the deal?

I didn't want to walk out of that cornfield too soon. I had so many hurts to remember.

As I walked up and down the rows of corn, I took the time to remember what I had to remember, and I must tell you the process was so bittersweet.

I came back onto the baseball field just as the sun was setting. Talk about a Hollywood ending.

When you are at that ball field in Iowa, and you come walking out of the cornfield, no one asks you why you have tears in your eyes. They know.

OK. Now that I have everyone in tears, let me tell you how I happened to be out in a field in Iowa.

KLYV, a real powerhouse of a station in Dubuque, had a morning drive team of Joe Dawson and Doug Collins. I had been speaking to them and their nice listeners for quite some time, and they came up with the wonderful idea that I should come there and cohost a show with them.

Pretty heady stuff. They bought me a round-trip airplane ticket (I guess they didn't want me to settle there) and of course booked me into a real nice motel.

I know it was real nice because it had a complimentary breakfast with little boxes of cold cereal and fruit. There was something also that they called "sweet rolls."

Doesn't anyone in Iowa know about a bagel with a schmear?

There are some other things I quickly learned about Iowa on that trip. First of all, it is flat. I mean really flat. And it is big. Really big.

When Doug was driving me out to see the Field of Dreams, I said to him that I hoped we didn't run into any traffic.

He broke up laughing, and I soon found out why. We were lucky to see another car on those roads. Some traffic problem they have. They call that driving? I would have had to hunt for another car to bump into.

Another thing was that everyone there seemed to look alike. Maybe it isn't politically correct to go down the following path, but I don't really care.

In New York City we have, for instance, one million kids in a thousand schools, speaking one hundred and sixty-seven languages, who are every shade of skin color possible. The diversity is unbelievable.

Don't get me wrong. I love those Iowa people. It's just that they all look so clean and neat and smell nice.

Anyway, it was a great treat for their listeners to arrive at the radio station and get to meet me. Ladies gave me the keys to their rooms. Men offered to buy me cars and boats. Well, not quite, but the reception was terrific.

It was just as fantastic as the trip I previously had to Birmingham, Alabama.

Stop the book. How did I just go from Dubuque, Iowa, to Birmingham, Alabama? Let me explain.

Before the Dubuque trip, I had been invited to Birmingham, Alabama, to do the same thing. Spend the morning hanging out with the two hosts of the morning drive show on WERC, Tommy Charles and John Ed.

The reason I started this chapter off with the Dubuque story was because I liked that business about the Field of Dreams. You must admit it did have a great deal of schmaltz. (Look elsewhere in this book for the meaning of that word. I don't want to repeat myself.)

In case you are lost, let me clear it up for you in simple terms.

The Birmingham trip was first. The Dubuque trip was second. I am telling the stories in reverse order. Got it straight?

In addition to being invited to Birmingham for the radio stuff, Tommy Charles was also having me down there so I could attend his daughter's wedding.

Listen up, folks. You got here the case of being invited to not only share a microphone with a legend in the broadcast world but also to attend his daughter's wedding. Not bad, wouldn't you say?

Tommy Charles and John Ed took me all around Birmingham and introduced me to everyone who was anyone. The wedding reception was at The Club, which is pronounced in Birmingham "thee" not "the."

Pronouncing it wrong is like calling Sixth Avenue in New York City, the Avenue of the Americas. It immediately shows who the out-of-towner is.

I got to meet all the good old boys that Tommy and John hang out with, and I must say, they were very cordial to this damn Yankee. As a matter of fact, they tolerated my request to see their pickup trucks.

To tell the truth, the line "y'all come back now" started to get on my nerves, and at one point I asked Tommy Charles if these guys were for real. He assured me that they were.

Tommy had asked a friend of his to loan me a Rolls Royce so I could drive around town. Even though it wasn't yellow, I took it.

Wow! Driving around Birmingham in a Rolls Royce. I could get used to that kind of living. All that it needed was an on-duty light on the roof and a meter in the front with me, and I would have been open for business.

Southern folk have a certain style to them, and it carries over into the types of stories that they tell. I brought this one back to the Big Apple, and I should like to share it with you.

Two good old boys had been fishing on the same river for more than thirty years. They were Zeke and Efron.

One day as they were doing the usual under a bridge, waiting for the fish to meet the frying pans, a funeral procession passed above. Zeke suddenly stopped, stood up straight, took his hat off his head, and didn't move an inch until the procession was completely out of sight.

Efron said, "Zeke, we have been fishing for thirty years, and never, not never, in all that time, have you ever stopped and done something like that. I just don't understand you."

"Friend," Zeke replied, "I was married to that woman for thirty-three years, and the least I could do was to show a little respect as she went by."

I could tell you more tales of my adventures in other cities around the United States done under similar situations where talk show hosts wanted me to come and visit their radio stations.

Since I am not getting paid by the word, I'll give you only one more example of how this broadcasting business brought me some traveling time.

It wasn't just big cities like Dubuque and Birmingham (well, the people living there think they are big cities, and who am I to let them know that they are not), it was also places like Altoona, Pennsylvania.

The station there is WFBG, and the morning drive guy is Sean McKay. He originally comes from someplace out west like Montana or Wyoming.

How he got to Altoona is not known to me, but he has become a fixture in that town as if he owned it. Maybe he does, come to think of it.

GO WEST, YOUNG MAN!
(to Altoona?)

Went looking for Billy Joel

Allentown

⊛ Altoona

Susquehanna River

Philadelphia

Went looking for W.C. Fields

Getting to Altoona was more my style of transportation. I was able to drive there. The adventure was just as nice as in all the other places I have been to visit.

The station had been running a promotional jingle for days before that I was to arrive. The local television station was there to do a story about me. I was given food and drink, and when it was time for me to drive back to New York City my vehicle was filled with goodies to eat on the trip back.

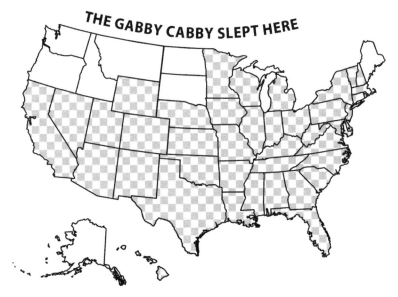

THE GABBY CABBY SLEPT HERE

You see, thanks to broadcasting adventures like this one, I got to learn that people all over the country want you to "eat, eat, eat." I used to think that it was only my mother and my grandmother who wanted me to eat all the time.

I enjoyed meeting the town's mayor, and when I put my arm around his honor, I said quite seriously, "I have brought you a gift from the mayor of New York City."

The mayor looked at me, anxiously waiting to find out what his gift would be. I told him I had brought to him from New York City, on behalf of the mayor—nine hundred illegal aliens.

As I drove back to the Big Apple later that night, I thought to myself, I was having an awful lot of fun because of this radio business.

I remember specifically, a few days after the Altoona trip, I was in my cab, and I talked about the trips I had gone on to a passenger who was a Madison Avenue advertising executive type.

He told me that it wasn't a big deal. Lots of New York City taxi drivers had probably done the same thing, he said.

I knew I was home, and I had a real New Yorker in the back of the hack.

This Chapter Has Some Sex—Put the Children to Sleep Before You Read It

S ome girls have all the pretty things while others have nothing," sniffed Amy.[7]

I'll never forget the time that Amy and her three sisters came to New York City and got into my cab. I am glad that there were only four of the March sisters. If there had been five, they would have had a problem. By law, a cab in the Big Apple can transport no more than four passengers.

Did I just hear you say to yourself, "I hope he will tell us about some of the real people who have been passengers in his yellow mobile conveyance lounge?"

Curl up in that comfy chair and read on.

Think about this. When I am driving, I am picking up a new person or persons every few minutes. They get into my cab and talk to me like they would talk to their bartender or shrink. The difference is they talk to the back of my head.

Sometimes, if there is more than one passenger, they talk to each other. If I am not being included in the conversation,

---

[7]*Little Women*; Louisa May Alcott; Waldman and Son

I can lean slightly back and hear everything that is being said. You didn't really know that cabdrivers, especially this one, listen in on your very personal conversations? Get smart.

I remember the two girls I took to Eighty-sixth Street. That is where there happens to be a number of psychologists. So when I am given that as a destination, I just know it is going to be a good ride.

Believe it or not, there are some people in New York City who have more money than they know what to do with, and if they can't spend ninety dollars an hour to find out they hate their mother, life isn't satisfying.

Contemplate that. How many people are there in your town who have more money than they know what to do with? In New York City, we have an abundance of them while the rest of the world is worrying about how to pay the rent.

Anyway, the two girls are chatting about whether or not they should have sex with their boyfriends. They completely forgot that I was in the cab with my ears burning. I was not being included in the discussion, they thought.

Back and forth it went. The reasons to have sex, the reasons not to have sex. And then for a change of pace, the reasons not to have sex and the reasons to have sex.

When we finally reached our destination, I was exhausted. Look, I know I am a pretty sexy guy who has some stamina, but just how much sex can one endure?

At one point in the ride, I had lost count of the number of possible sexual encounters that had been talked about. I felt physically drained, and although I do not smoke, I desperately needed a cigarette.

Was it as good for them as it was for me?

They paid the fare, added a small tip (young ladies are terrible tippers), and as they walked away toward their appointment with the shrink, I realized that I got about four bucks for what he was going to get one hundred and eighty. Life is not fair or should I say fare.

Then there was the time when "she" got into my taxi. This was one good-looking babe. My heart started to pound, and in a flash I was in a scene in *From Here to Eternity* where Burt Lancaster ravishes Deborah Kerr on the sand. My palms began to sweat. Would this passenger ask me up to her apartment in lieu of the fare? Maybe there would be a little muffky fuffky, if you catch my drift.

Ladies and Gentlemen and Children, a short public service announcement at this time, please. This event took place before I was married and prior to the days of HIV and AIDS. In those days, you could fantasize and then maybe do it. Today, you can fantasize, but you can't do it.

So boys and girls who have their hearts set on growing up to be cabdrivers, just remember that it is not a good idea to do you know what with your passengers.

Come to think of it, thinking about the tips some of them give me, they are doing it to me already.

Back to the tale.

"She," it turns out, was not a "she." My heart was broken and my daydream ripped apart. You know how they do it in the movies. Suddenly the film just rips across the screen and you are back to reality.

The guy was a transvestite, and he was in seventh heaven. His occupation was being a shoplifter, and according to him he had just reached the pinnacle of his career.

Can you imagine putting down on your tax return that you are a transvestite/shoplifter? I bet the folks at the tax office would fight over who gets the chance to audit that return.

The pinnacle, the acme, the top of his profession was getting arrested and then having the cops unsure whether a male cop or a female cop should do the examination for weapons, he explained.

Now stick with me on this. It gets a little complicated. If a male cop checks a transvestite/shoplifter, and it turns out to be a male, that is nothing.

If it is a male cop that does the checking, and it turns out that the person really is a girl, that is a great deal of fun.

But if it is a female cop, and this is what happened to my passenger, that checks the perpetrator out, and it turns out to be a male, that is fantastic.

My passenger claimed that the lady police officer touched his family jewels and said, "This is crazy."

I thought to myself this guy in the back of my cab was a real jerk. He was bragging to me about this adventure, but he had missed the great line of all time.

If I had been in his position at the police station, and a lady cop said to me that "This was crazy" when she touched me, I would have looked her in the eye and said,

"No, officer, this is nuts."

OK. I have now told you two stories dealing with sex. Since I want this book to be in the library at your local church or synagogue school, I will shift gears at this point.

I am cruising up fancy-schmantzie Park Avenue and I get hailed by a suit.

Two explanations at this point, dear reader. First, Park Avenue used to be called Fourth Avenue many years ago, and as a matter of fact on most official plans of sewers and subways and buildings, it still says that.

It was changed to Park Avenue so that the people who live there will think it is a big deal. Well, it happens to be a big deal because that is where a great many millionaires now live.

The apartment buildings have doormen, but what is really unbelievable is that many of them have elevator operators. When was the last time that you went to visit someone in an apartment house that had an elevator operator?

If you want to tweak a Park Avenue millionaire's wife, just tell her she really lives on Fourth Avenue.

The expression "suit" means that the person is some kind of a big shot. He wears a suit that has to be dry-cleaned, not one that you wash and hang up. I am not a "suit" for three reasons. I do not live on Park Avenue. I do not have the money to pay for dry cleaning. I do not have two items of clothing in my wardrobe that match.

Mr. Park Avenue Suit gets into the cab and tells me that he left his eyeglasses at his girlfriend's house last night, and he can hardly see me, much less do a day's work at his office.

He gives me the address of his babe and off we go. On the way, he makes small talk about the restaurant they had dinner in the night before, the movie they went to see, and the fact that he slept over at her house.

The restaurant was of no interest. I subsequently avoided seeing the movie based on his recommendation that I see it. As for him sleeping over at the girl's house, I knew the good Lord was probably punishing him (taking away his eyeglasses) for doing that when they weren't married.

Come to think of it, the good Lord was also punishing me by having me drive and listen to this guy's exploits. So boring I could have fallen asleep at the wheel. What kept me awake was that someone kept beeping their car horn as they drove through traffic.

Me.

I drop him off at his girl's house so he can go in and get his missing eyeglasses. Keep in mind that he was not really able to get a good look at me because of his vision problem. That has great significance in the next part of my tale.

Believe it or not (I don't have to make this stuff up, trust me), I get hailed by the same guy later in the day. The statistical possibility of that is one out of a gazillion or maybe even two gazillions.

Mr. Park Avenue Suit once again gets into my yellow mobile conveyance lounge, and keep in your mind he doesn't recognize me because he couldn't see me earlier in the day.

Before he gets a chance to say a word, I tell him that I am only driving a taxi temporarily.

"What is that you do when you aren't driving a cab?" he asks.

"I am studying to be a mind reader," I reply.

"No kidding," he says.

"Yup. And I am pretty good at," I reply.

"That is a great deal of crap. No one can do that," he says.

Suits think they know it all, so I tell him that for five bucks I can read his mind. He agrees. He figures he is about to get a free taxi ride.

I proceed to tell him where his girlfriend lives, what restaurant he likes, what movie he likes, and I do it in a dramatic way that would delight Marmaduke the Magician who knows all, sees all.

He is amazed. He is astounded. I mean Mr. Park Avenue Suit, not Marmaduke. Pay attention to my story.

He pays the fare and a small tip and then hands me the extra five bucks for reading his mind. He walks away from the taxi totally amazed at my psychic abilities.

The moral of this story is that college-educated corporate leaders in Manhattan who wear suits can outsmart a New York City taxi driver every time. Not quite.

Hang on for just a second, I want to count the number of words I have written so far in this chapter. I want to see if I have room for just one more delicious true tale. Let us see, the number of words is one thousand nine hundred thirty-six. It seems that I do have the room.

I pick up this couple at the Pennsylvania Railroad Station terminal, and they give me the address of their daughter up in Westchester. This is the county just north of New York City. A good fare.

Now these are two people who really looked straight to me. They didn't have orange hair, and they weren't wearing jewelry in their noses. Additionally, they were on their way to visit their child who was married and had a kid or two.

What we are talking about here is real American folk.

As we are putting the bags into my trunk, the guy says that he would like to have sex with his wife on the way to Westchester.

He explains that they have never done anything so silly or wild in their otherwise ordinary lives and that they had

63

discussed this on the train. Would I mind? They hoped that I would be understanding.

Understanding? Understanding? Not only did I suddenly become the most understanding cabdriver on the face of the Earth, I immediately began to calculate just how much I could see of the backseat area through my rearview mirror.

I figured that as long as they stayed on the seat and didn't sink to the floor of the cab, I was in for a good show. The ride to Westchester County would be about thirty-five minutes, I thought. If I could count on them to be, how shall I put this delicately?

ANIMALS.

I knew I was in for one heck of ride. I thanked the good Lord for my fortune, and off we went.

It was a good trip. It was a nice trip. I enjoyed that trip.

When we got to their daughter's house they got out of the cab. They thanked me for their ride (Which ride were they referring to?). The husband gave me an excellent tip (money) and handed me his business card.

I was going to ask him if he was giving me that card because he wanted me to recommend him to other passengers, but, instead, I asked him if I could give out his name and phone number to talk show hosts around the country so that they could call him and discuss the ride and the ride "on air."

Not to worry, I promised him, his name and telephone number would be given "off air." Mr. Grandfather Stud said he couldn't care less if they wanted to give his name "on air."

And so in the weeks that followed, a number of talk show hosts had the occasion to dial a telephone number in

Boca Raton, Florida, and find out just how it was to have a sexual experience in a New York City taxi.

I bet no listener turned off his or her radio during that interview.

Now you know why the radio audiences around the world are growing in numbers. Listeners love to have sex while hearing me tell a story about the couple that had sex in my taxi. That is what I call radio-active.

Having now finished that tale, the number of words for this chapter is at two thousand four hundred and sixty-one. That's enough.

The City With a Million Stories Hidden Behind a Million Windows— What a Great Place to Be a Glazier

Loudon Tripp, wearing a seersucker suit and a Harvard tie, sat in my office on a very nice day in September and told me he'd looked into my background and might hire me.

"Oh boy," I said.[8]

After he left the garage, I leaned back in my swivel chair with the black vinyl, lit a Czechoslovakian cigarette, loaded my Beretta, and screwed on its silencer.

I was ready for the streets. As I walked to the cab, I made sure I was not followed. Spenser would have done that.

Off in the distance, I could hear music which I immediately recognized as "Proud Mary."

Once again, I said those words which had become the fabric of my very existence. "The cab ride is not over until it is over."

---

[8] *Paper Dolls*; Robert B. Parker; Berkley Publishing

What the hell am I talking about? Does any of this make sense to you the reader? Well, it makes a great deal of sense to me since I am now getting paid by the word for this chapter.

When I do a night shift on the streets of New York, it's like being a character in a private detective novel. You just can't imagine how exciting it is to pull a cab out of a garage knowing that for the next twelve hours you are going to be part of a great adventure.

The early part of the evening is just the warm-up. This is when you take people home from work. This is when you take people to the theater. This is when you take people to dinner. The early evening crowd is not that much different from your day riders.

The adventure begins at about midnight. You not only get the action in the cab, but you also get the chance to check out activities generally unknown to the public.

Come on. Let me be your guide.

We go to the Port Authority Bus Terminal at about 2:30 A.M. It is at Forty-second Street and Eighth Avenue, an area that can conjure up your worst nightmares.

Port Authority? Port Authority? Yes, you remember, the folks who run the Central Taxi Hold filthy bathrooms at the airports. I am glad to see that you are paying attention to my stories.

Would it be real mean of me to say that the people who generally lurk in that area of the city in the wee hours of the morning are some of the strangest-looking people in the world? Maybe mean, but it's the truth.

Let us walk to gate number eighteen, and you will see a sight that will really upset you if you have one ounce of humanity inside of you.

This is where the bus leaves for Attica. For those of you who have not spent time in the slammer and do not know of such things, this is a tough prison in upstate New York. To get sent there, you really have to be one piece of work.

It is a prison where people who rob and kill grandmothers are sent. It is the place where men who rape a girl and smash in her face with a brick are sent. It is the place where they have people who are worse than the monsters in a horror show.

Do you get my point? A very bad place is Attica.

The women and children who mull around gate eighteen for hours and hours are the wives, the girlfriends, the mothers, the sisters, and the children of the prisoners. They go to that gate to take an eight-hour bus trip to Attica.

Can you believe it? Those bus riders still love the prisoners who have destroyed not only their own lives but also their own families.

At the bus terminal, every bus line that uses the place must pay a hefty ransom to the Port Authority. Guess what? All buses coming into New York City are required to use that terminal.

If you haven't grasped it yet, we are talking big money here.

How come, then, the women and children at gate eighteen have to stand for hours with no place to sit? How come there is no place to change a diaper? How come there is no toilet open at that time of night?

I think what gets you the most is their eyes. You look into their eyes as they wait there and you see such pain and sadness. It can break your heart. They are guilty only of hooking up with some bad characters, and for that they are going to pay and pay some more.

The crowd, by the way, is all Black and Hispanic. The only neat- and clean-looking people that you see around are the Port Authority Police.

Finally, the bus pulls into its spot and a very abusive Black man addresses the crowd.

"We are going to do this my way and my way alone. Anybody who gives me a hard time stays here."

Talk about a crummy way to say hello.

And so the herd of people is moved toward the bus for the long trip upstate. You don't see the excitement and happiness that you would see in people who are on their way to some vacation destination.

There are no suitcases. All that you see are shabby paper and plastic shopping bags. Certainly none with the name of a fine department store.

You continue to see the eyes. Sad eyes. Tired eyes. And no matter how much you know where these people are going, it just breaks your heart to look upon such a sight.

They will do the trip, spend some time visiting at the prison, and they will do the return trip back to New York City.

Whew. Let's get out of here. I am starting to sound like some kind of social scientist. Get in the back of my hack and let me find a place for us to eat.

I know. Let us go over to the Market Diner. It's open twenty-four hours a day, seven days a week, three hundred and sixty-five days a year. Hmm. Sounds like the hours of a cab company.

Let me explain. In the old days, when railroads were king, they had dining cars on them so the folks going here and there could eat like a bunch of swells rather than munching on a sandwich at their seat.

On some trains, they were quite splendid. Well, with the demise of that kind of rail travel in the United States, many of the dining cars were taken off the tracks, placed on cement blocks, and used as roadside restaurants alongside this newfangled method of getting someplace called "highways."

Excuse me for gloating, but I love hearing stories about roads winning over tracks. What possible fun is there in riding in something that has to stick to miles of steel?

Wheeling and dealing through vehicle traffic, now that's the game.

"Yo! Putz. (Remember, I told you what that means.) Whadda you want to do, take off some of my paint?"

The Market Diner isn't one of those old railroad cars, but it is done in that style. It has its own parking lot, and that is important—just as important as the fact that it has a bathroom to use.

A cabdriver's dream. A place to park where you can eat and pee. It just doesn't get any better than that.

Come on, we'll get a bagel with a schmear and a cup of coffee. We will schmooze with the other drivers. We will exchange stories. We will complain about the cops.

Then we will make another pee and get back on the road. But first, I better explain "schmooze" to you. There are two ways to talk.

One way is not moving your arms while you talk, and the other way is moving them while you talk. When you schmooze you move your arms. Otherwise you are just talking, not schmoozing.

On the road again we go. The steam comes up from the streets. Every out-of-towner wants to know what it is.

If it is just floating up softly then it is only the heat from what is below the city's streets. The subways, the water pipes, the steam pipes, the telephone lines, the television cable lines, the sewers are all down there.

The steam coming up with real force means that there is probably a steam pipe leaking down there, and someone is going to have to go down into that inferno to fix it.

Look over there at that hooker. She is probably fourteen years old.

My goodness, did you see the car wreck we just passed? It will be gone from that intersection by the time we get back as packs of tow trucks attack.

Can you see that pile of horse manure over there? That comes from the mounted cops who definitely do not pick up after their horses. For your historical information, that was exactly the reason our sanitation department was originally formed so many years ago.

It was the job of the sanitation department to go after horse manure. Only in later years did anyone figure that we might as well let them also pick up the garbage.

People realized that the horse doo-doo was quite valuable to city terrace and roof gardeners, and they would go out of their way to buy it. The city fathers began to sell it to the gardeners. Just think, a city where people will buy shit.

And in case you are wondering, the sanitation department still has the joy of picking up the doo-doo unless a gardener grabs it first. Just think, a city where people steal shit.

Our next stop is "The Tunnel." I am pretty sure Junior Vasquez will be there this morning. You don't know who he is? You don't know what "The Tunnel" is?

Listen. New York City has all these very "in" clubs where you stand in line outside and pray that the doorman who looks like King Kong will let you come in.

He walks down the line and actually picks and chooses who he thinks is acceptable. It is crueler and meaner than any college fraternity initiation you ever heard of.

If you are lucky, and I mean real lucky, you just might get picked. It doesn't hurt to have purple hair with a tattoo on your forehead, by the way.

So we get picked because I am the maestro of the city streets and in we go. Hundreds of flashing lights, blaring music, human shapes twisting here and there on the dance floor. Who owns this place, a guy called Dante maybe?

Junior Vasquez is up on the mezzanine running his records in a style that has given him thousands of devoted fans. For the participants this scene is a dream fulfilled. For a mother, it is probably the worst nightmare possible.

Which, of course, reminds me of the following story.

A young white girl from a small Midwest town comes to New York City to find her fame and fortune. When she left home she told her scrub clean friends, relatives, and associates that she was going to make it to the top in the Big Apple in, let us say, being an insurance actuary.

I don't have anything against insurance people, by the way. I am just using that as example because actuaries live by the words, "God forbid you should die," "God forbid your house should burn down," and "God forbid you should have a car crash."

You think they worry about you? No. They worry that their company will have to pay a claim if one of those things happens to you. "God forbid they should have to pay a claim."

So the girl from the Midwest takes up with a Black guy and goes dancing at places like The Tunnel every night. She gets pregnant.

Not because she is dancing, silly, but because she is sleeping with the colored guy. Did I really have to explain that?

The girl calls home to tell her beloved mother about the situation she is in.

"Ma. I have some news for you."

"Yes my darling daughter, what is it?"

"I am no longer in the insurance business. I now dress strange, look strange, and dance to all hours of the morning."

The mother pauses for a few seconds and says, "For myself I don't care."

Then the daughter proceeds to say, "I am living with a Black man."

"For myself, I don't care," replies the mother.

By this time the kid is beginning to wonder why her mother seems to be taking this so well.

"And one other thing, Ma. The Black man has made me pregnant."

"For myself I don't care," is said again by the mother.

To which the young girl says, "Ma. I don't understand. I have told you all these things which I thought for sure you would get upset and angry about, and yet you continue to say, 'For myself, I don't care.'"

Ma replied, "I am saying 'for myself, I don't care' because I am going to throw myself off the top of the barn and land on a pitchfork."

It is starting to get light, so I usually head over to the Plaza Hotel where I am sure to get a fare that is going out to Newark Airport. This is a good fare because you get what is on the meter plus ten dollars. You get that because you are not, as a New York City cabdriver, allowed to pick up a return fare at that airport which is in New Jersey.

I usually get to the hotel before the doormen arrive for work, and I find it fascinating that once they put on their uniforms with all the braids and all the shiny buttons they look like a big deal. In their ordinary clothes, however, they look just like cabdrivers.

For many years, I have studied the various rituals of bellhops and doormen at many hotels. I offer you one at this time.

When you are checking out, the bellhop comes to your room and gets your bags. He will not, however, bring them over to my cab. He will leave them with the doorman.

You now give the bellhop a tip and he walks off. Then, the doorman picks up the bags and puts them into the trunk of my cab.

Then, dear hotel guest, you are trapped into giving the doorman a tip also.

Once, years ago, I tried to help a doorman with the bags, and he warned me that if I didn't leave them alone he would put a suitcase in my ear.

I have a feeling that if all the tips that are glommed out of visitors to New York City were sent instead to Washington, D.C., this country would have no national debt.

Got to stop talking. Got to drive the cab. Got to go make some money. You come back for the next chapter.

The Trouble With New York City Is That There Is No Place to Eat or Spend Money

There were only a few customers scattered around the tables, since it was nearly nine thirty and by that hour, the clientele were inside, busy with the perdrix en casserole or tournedos Beauharnais[9]...

I decided to go take a look at the kitchen. I wanted to know if I was eating in a restaurant that had a kitchen in which you could eat off the floor it was so clean.

Now in most places in the world, if you ask to check out an eating place's kitchen, you are asking for a meat cleaver in the head or at the very least a rolling pin in the gotchkiss.

However, in New York City, there actually is a law that you have the right to examine the kitchen of the restaurant that you are in.

Surprise. Surprise. The notice of that is not posted in any New York City restaurant that I know of. And, you better be careful how you handle that, right? Need I tell you that sometimes there is a long distance between the law and its actual implementation.

---

[9] *The Black Moutain*; Rex Stout; Penguin Books

Food and the eating thereof, is the defining aspect of a people. It certainly is the defining aspect of people living in the Big Apple.

The two main occupations of the citizens of my city, and the visitors to it, are spending money on eating and the buying of some type of merchandise.

Far and away, the most important thing in this town is Mr. Green (money). You either give it to someone or you get it from someone. A third possibility is that you take it away from someone, but that can be very risky here.

I say risky because although it is a mandatory one-year jail sentence for having a gun in your pocket, many ordinary people do carry them. I am talking about lawyers, teachers, doctors. Thus, try to rob a person, and you might find yourself looking down the barrel of the victim's gun.

When I was in jail (discussed more fully in another chapter), I remember a cell block mate complaining to me that he was shot by the person he was holding up.

As the perpetrator, he had a knife, and he felt that the victim was unfair to whip out a 9mm automatic and shoot him. I explained the concept of occupational hazard to him.

Come to think of it, wouldn't it be really neat if I could combine the subjects of food and crime for you in a nice joke? So, I will.

This is about the gangster who gets riddled with bullets on a New York City street and he drags himself over to his mother's house.

Being riddled with bullets is uncomfortable, messy, and it hurts. Dragging is not so good either.

He finally gets to his mother's house, crawls up the steps, rings the doorbell, and when she opens the door he says, "Momma, Momma, I have been shot by the Nunzio brothers."

The Nunzio brothers were, by the way, Pasquale and Arivedeci.

She looks at her son. He is one big mess. The bullets, the blood, his rumpled suit. It is every mother's nightmare.

He tries to speak to his mother.

"Shh," she says, "have something to eat. We will talk later."

I hope you noticed how I avoided using the typical Mafia story line. I could have said he was an Italian gangster, and it was in Little Italy where he was shot.

That technique was omitted because I am sick and tired of all gangsters and their shootings in New York City being portrayed as Italian incidents. I find it offensive, and if there really were a Mafia in my city, why upset them by telling you an Italian joke, which they might read?

This is why I want you to know that Pasquale and Arivedeci Nunzio were two Jewish guys.

Getting back to food as a defining aspect. If you had to talk about New York City as a house, its kitchen would be its streets. I am not just talking about the restaurants, I am also talking about the vendors.

I love giving numbers out about New York City. Like there are a million kids in a thousand schools speaking 167 languages. Like there are 60,000 cabdrivers. Like there are 28,000 people in the slammer. You want numbers, I got numbers.

So, would it surprise you to know that on a nice sunny day in the Big Apple, there are more than nine thousand people on the streets selling food?

You can buy Chinese noodles and dumplings, calzones, pizzas, Jewish knishes, German bratwurst, Indian samosas, Argentine empanadas, Japanese yakitori, Caribbean rotti, and Philippine lumpia.

How about soft pretzels, crab rolls, charlotte russes, fresh muffins, corn tacos, broiled corn, and Philadelphia cheese steaks?

Philadelphia? How did that get in there? What can I tell you? That is what we call our street steaks. Notice I said "our."

You see, getting robbed or even murdered are minor dangers to me as I drive my yellow mobile conveyance lounge.

The real threat I have faced all these years is becoming fat. How do you stop eating when there is someone on every corner who is willing to push food into you? And, by the way, I am going to tell you a secret about those guys. Please don't tell anyone else. Let this be our little secret.

They charge cabdrivers less than they charge you.

So, I guess if you want to save money on eats when you come to New York City, drive around in a yellow car and don't speak English so well.

The three questions I am asked the most about food in my city are:

What's a good restaurant?

Is it safe to buy food from one of those street vendors?

What is a knish?

The question, "What is a good restaurant?" is kind of difficult so we shall let that wait a bit while I answer the other two questions.

A knish is ... Golly, this is not going to be easy without using my hands. Let me think about this for a second. Come to think of it, maybe I should just go buy one and show you what it looks like.

Before I go and get us a couple of knishes, keep in mind that it is a staple of a New Yorker's diet. They are sold on the streets by the vendors. Almost every vendor who is selling any type of food, no matter what the nationality is, also sells a knish.

Yes, a Japanese guy selling sushi will also sell a knish. A Middle East guy selling falafel will also sell a knish.

You wait here. I will be back shortly.

While I am gone, do the following test.

1. Who are the Knickerbockers?
2. Who was the first vice president of the United States to be cremated?
3. Where was the first sidewalk built?
4. Was Mae West ever in the Gabby Cabby taxi?
5. What was the "Borscht Belt"?
6. What is the connection between New York City and Captain William Kidd?

I am back. How did you do on the test? You can find the answers at the end of this chapter.

Here are the two knishes that I bought. Notice that they look like small pillows that can fit into the palm of your hand. Consider the outside sort of like the pillowcase. It has a crusty, breadedlike texture.

Inside, which you might call the stuffing for the pillow, is the mashed potato containing secret ingredients that get your taste buds nuts.

The vendor splits the knish sideways and pushes in a glob of mustard. Oh, my Lord! I am dripping saliva on my chin just talking about it.

Have your knish now. Here it is.

While you are eating the knish, let me tell you about a suggestion I make to folks who are coming to the Big Apple and are afraid of being accosted by some bad person because that is what Hollywood and the television have led them to believe.

Knish shortly before it's final stage

Now I am not working for the chamber of commerce, but I got to tell you that according to the Federal Bureau of Investigation, New York City is the safest large city in the United States. We aren't even on the list of the top seventy cities when it comes to crime. Believe me.

But just like you can't convince some people that flying is safe, you can't convince some people that New York City is safe. So to those people, I give the following advice.

As you walk about on our streets, scratch yourself and drool saliva. No one will bother you.

Finish your knish and let us move on.

The answer to the question, "Is it safe to buy food from one of those street vendors?" is a qualified yes.

If the particular vendor that you are considering giving some of your money to looks like he was just dragged out of the Black Hole of Calcutta, I would suggest keeping your bucks in your pocket and moving on to one who knows what a bar of soap is used for.

By the way, this advice has nothing to do with you getting sick. Honestly, I don't know of any cases of someone getting ill from eating food that was sold on the streets of New York City.

It's just that when your hot dog also smells like the person who sold it to you, well, that is just not too pleasant.

Come. Eat. You'll be fine.

Now, to the number-one question I am asked concerning food here.

What's a good restaurant?

The reason that this is a tough one is because there are just so many. I always like to make the point that it would really be tough to be a crummy restaurant and stay in business in New York City.

My advice is to explore. Take a gamble. Be daring.

But if you really pressed me about my own personal favorite, this is what I would answer. I love my wife's restaurant (our family kitchen) the best.

As for restaurants that are not operated in my kitchen, my suggestion this week might not necessarily be my suggestion next week. I am not fickle. It is just that chefs change, menus change, seasons change.

Invite me to dinner (with you paying), and on that day I shall have a really super eating place picked out for you. Make sure you bring Mr. Green also.

If you don't want to take me to dinner, check out my Web site (http://gabby.com) which has some eating ideas that will be current on the day you check it out.

And now you can't-wait-to-spend-some-money readers, let us do a little time together talking about buying things in New York City. As a way of introducing this topic, we really should first talk about selling things.

I like to tell visitors to the Big Apple, let's say they come from Jackson, Mississippi, that if they had cleaned out their attic, and brought a great deal of that junk along with them, we could set up a table on a street corner and make a fortune selling "genuine Confederate artifacts."

Probably one of the reasons that crime is comparatively low in New York City is that more money is to be made by selling T-shirts on a street than robbing people.

On the average day, about fifty thousand people will walk past the average corner in midtown Manhattan. That is a pretty good clientele for a business to have.

In addition, we are talking about a business that does not pay taxes.

My goodness. Have I surprised someone? Were you under the impression that a vendor selling purses for ladies or wallets for men on the street was filing a tax form at the end of the year? Yeah, right.

And let me tell you another thing about New York City and all this street selling. If that couple from Mississippi had really brought that stuff from the attic to sell, they would have had a blast doing it.

I don't care how much money you make in your regular job, there is a real kick in selling something to someone and keeping all the money without having the government as your partner.

As for the counterfeit things that you have heard so much about. How would you like to look at my gold fifteen-thousand-dollar watch? I always get a new one when my wrist starts to turn green.

The variety of items that are for sale just blows your mind. I love to tell the following:

You have a garage door opener and you need one little part for it.

You search from one end of the world to the other trying to find it.

You can't.

You come to New York City and walk into a small shop down on Canal Street and tell the guy your problem.

He asks you, "What color do you want?"

Canal Street has another distinction, by the way. It crosses Manhattan from the East River to the Hudson River. At one end you have the Manhattan Bridge and at the other end you have the Holland Tunnel. It is probably the biggest single driving nightmare street in New York City.

We have motorists using Canal Street to go home to Brooklyn, and we have the motorists going home to New Jersey. Certainly, when they finally do get home, they will complain about the number of cars in Manhattan.

Our big department stores are, of course, fantastic, but for really interesting shopping you not only hit them you also go into the various ethnic areas for unusual bargains.

I am talking about going up to Spanish Harlem for sneakers. I am talking about going to the Garment Center where you can get clothing wholesale (for cash).

Keep in mind they don't make the clothing here as much as they used to, but the showrooms and offices are still here dictating what much of America will be wearing next season.

New York City ladies generally operate in a pack. In the group, one lady knows where to buy dresses, one knows where to get sweaters, one knows where to get coats. You know what I mean when I say pack, don't you? Like in a feeding frenzy, and in this case we are not thinking of food.

Why do they get it for cash? Golly. I don't know why a businessperson would want to make some cash sales. Do you?

Garment Center? Time for another joke. What can I say? I love being the star of this book.

Two ladies are walking on the street in the middle of the Garment Center, and one says to the other, "Mrs. Klopman, that is the most beautiful diamond ring I have ever seen."

To which Mrs. Klopman responds with a long face, "Yes, but it comes with the Klopman curse."

The other lady says, "The Klopman curse? What is that?"

To which Mrs. Klopman answers, "The Klopman curse is Mr. Klopman."

I am on a roll. Let me give you another Garment Center joke.

You got these two partners who year after year lose money because they always pick out the wrong fabric. They never seem to be able to guess what is going to be in next season.

They pick cotton. Wool is in.

They pick white. Blue is in.

One partner can't stand it any longer and decides he is going to kill himself because they are so deeply in debt. He goes to the roof of the building where they have their showroom and throws himself off.

Hurtling down to certain death, he looks in the windows of his competitors.

As he passes the second floor where his company has an office, just seconds away from splat, he yells into his partner, "Buy velvet."

Buying merchandise in New York City, whether it be on the street or in a showroom or in a real store, is an adventure. As with my comments about picking out a restaurant for you, telling you the current hot place to shop is tough because things change so fast around here.

My point in this chapter was just to stimulate your palate for eating and get your chest pounding for spending.

But remember, the first buck you spend should be with me. I have a receding hairline, I wear glasses, I am about six feet tall, I weigh about one hundred and ninety pounds, and I am the guy driving the yellow car.

Bring me Mr. Green, sweetheart ...

The answers to the test are:

1. It was the name given to the original Dutch settlers. Now it is used by a bunch of tall guys who play basketball in their shorts at Madison Square Garden.

2. Nelson Rockefeller, who was a governor of the state of New York went on to become vice president of the United

States, and when he died they cremated him. Can you imagine that being the big thing in a person's life—or should I say death?

3. Gosh. Let me see. I know. The first sidewalk in the United States was built in New York City in 1657, and it was called "Stone Street." No, it was not paved with gold.

4. Mae West was a New York City babe who made good. This orginal sexpot was never in my cab, but her granddaughter Madonna was.

5. The "Borscht Belt" was what they called the Catskill Mountain resorts that are just north of New York City. It doesn't really exist anymore, and I feel sad that I never was able to perform there. I mean telling jokes. I don't mean driving a cab, silly.

6. Captain William Kidd, the pirate, was a New York City resident prior to becoming the terror of the high seas. For that matter, so was Al Capone a resident prior to moving to Chicago. Today our "bad guys" snatch purses from little old ladies and they think they are criminals. Big deal.

Clean up Your Room. Why Don't You Help Your Mother? Isn't Your Homework Done Yet? Kids Just Drive You Nuts

T om!"

No answer.

"Tom!"

No answer.

"What's gone with that boy, I wonder? You Tom!"[10]

Children are supposed to grow up. It can be along the Mississippi River or it can be watching a tree grow in Brooklyn. The same is for boys and girls.

They are supposed to be kids and then teenagers and then young adults and then old and pruned.

And all along the way, they are really absolutely positively supposed to be your biggest pain in the ass, your biggest worry, and maybe every once in a while that certain something that makes life worth living. When you see your kid get up and play the piano at the school play or kick the winning goal or pitch the no-hitter, now that is living.

---

[10] *The Adventures of Tom Sawyer*; Mark Twain; Watermill Press

There is one thing that children are definitely not supposed to do, however. That something they are absolutely, definitely, positively not supposed to do is to die before their parents.

I have often thought that there should be a special staircase to heaven for parents who later in their own lives, pass away and then ascend to meet a child who so long ago died, much too early.

One of the really neat things about this radio broadcasting for stations all over the world is that I found myself with a twenty-four-hour-a-day, seven-day-a week telephone.

Most people know that they will get most of their phone calls from the outside world from about daybreak to midnight. After that, the proper person does not dial your digits.

Also, the calls you receive on a Saturday and a Sunday are usually very different from the ones that you receive during the week. Business discussions during the week, relatives and friends on the weekend.

Well, not in my case. As the radio-active cabby, I started getting phone calls from radio people at all hours of the night and on weekends. Keep in mind that the middle of the night in New York City is an afternoon someplace else. Sunday in the Big Apple is a Monday someplace else.

Ring. Ring. Ring.

Who will that be? Maybe some guy from a Beijing station. Or is it Pretoria in South Africa? Could be an early arrival at a station in Boise, Idaho?

What a kick. I never know who is going to call next.

One time there was a call from a lady from the Children's Wish Foundation of Canada. The father of a child who was not doing too well, had heard me on CJOB in Winnipeg, and because his child had the "wish" of coming to New York City, wondered if I could be the driver and the guide?

A number of things quickly passed through my mind. Every parent's worst nightmare. Knowing that your child is very sick.

I wondered what kind of a kid would pick New York City instead of Disney World for such a wish?

Could I spend the day with a family under that type of stress?

Was the lady who was speaking to me, thinking I was going to do it for nothing? How much would they pay? Should I ask them for money, or did they think I was going to volunteer my services?

Well, I figured that I could only find out the answer to the "What kind of a kid... " and "Could I spend the day..." if I actually did it.

As for the money, I said before being asked that I would do it for half my usual rate.

I think I said that because somehow I wanted to be doing something right, but at the same time, I wasn't in the financial situation where I could work for nothing.

The Children's Wish lady agreed and said that she would send me an itinerary for the family. I suggested that maybe I should telephone the child in Winnipeg so that he would feel that he knew me a little before he got to New York City. I didn't want to be just a radio voice to him.

So I called and I spoke to the dad and the mom and the young man. It was such a strange feeling I had when I got off the phone. They just seemed to be like everyone else.

I felt a little better about the whole deal. Nothing was going to be different about this job than any other except for the fact that one of my passengers was going to be a child in rather poor health.

Talk about being nervous. On the day, I went to pick up the family, after they arrived in New York City, I really was concerned. I was afraid that I would show my own uncomfortable feeling and somehow mess up their trip.

I quickly learned that families that have a very ill child do not necessarily walk around with that grief showing every minute. That doesn't mean that they don't care. It's just that they learn to live with it.

That first day I learned to live with it also.

I took them here, there, and everywhere. This kid wanted New York City. I was going to give him New York City.

One particular incident really stands out in my mind. I took the family to Coney Island, and while they were walking on the beach and I was standing on the boardwalk, I noticed that the young man was away from mom, dad, sister, and brother.

I found that by holding up my hand to block him from my sight, he was no longer in the scene. It was the ocean, the beach, the family, but not him.

What I was doing, I guess, was trying to see what the scene would look like without him. Sort of a preview of another day.

OK. So what's the message here? You got me. I can't for the life of me come up with some profound thought as to why it was meant for that boy to die at such an early age, and die he did a number of months later back home in Canada.

But that first youngster, and there have been more after, got me into another whole aspect of this broadcasting business. I found myself being a part of a wish. If that isn't enough to teach you the difference between everyday problems and a big one, I don't know what is.

Let me do a little pontificating here and be quite serious for a minute. I hope I have done enough to make you laugh in the other chapters.

When I first started doing the broadcasting, it was a lark, and I didn't really do much heavy thinking about it. As time passed, and I began to realize that I was bringing some fun and some humor through my true tales to people all over the world, I realized that I had picked up a responsibility that I hadn't bargained for.

In many instances, I was even being asked by the talk show hosts what my opinion was about a particular social problem or event.

I found myself having the opportunity to say things that I believe in. I told millions of people that I think the health care system in the United States leaves a great many people out in the cold. It bothered me, I told my listeners, that there were people in this country who had to make a choice between rent and medicine.

I said that as a parent I had found that it doesn't pay to be permissive with your kids. Sure, you love them, but you got to be tough to keep them straight. Don't be afraid of "losing their love."

I told Australian audiences that it was crummy for the French to start testing nuclear bombs down there. I told the audience in Hong Kong that I didn't think that they really had much to fear when the People's Republic of China regains control of that community.

If I was asked, I spoke up. When did you run into a cab-driver who didn't have a mouth? My advantage was that I had millions and millions of ears that were listening and still are.

It became clear to me as time went on that I must be careful to treat this deal with a great amount of respect and that I should try very hard not to do anything that would betray the trust people seem to be putting in me.

There are, from time to time, some talk show hosts who try to get me to give the bad about New York City. They want to hear about the murders and the robberies and the muggings.

My standard answer is that I am not working for the chamber of commerce, but I got to tell you that the Big Apple is a really nice place and not something you should be afraid to come visit.

I also make the observation that people tell other people not to come to New York City because it is dangerous or that we are unfriendly. It is very unfair to stop some-one from having a wonderful time in the greatest city in the world.

Now let me give you a couple of true tales that show that even a child who is getting kicked in the ass by life can experience something very unique in my city.

One of the young people who came to New York City was in very difficult circumstances. He was in a motorized wheelchair, had little control over anything and was even accompanied by a specially trained dog who was sort of his companion and watcher.

My job was to drive his family's specially equipped van that had an electric lift for moving him in and out of the vehicle.

One day we went to the Statue of Liberty, and I had to pull the van right up to where the boats leave to cross the harbor. The people at the gangplank were very courteous and helpful.

As the boat moved away from the dock, I was approached by two New York City Park Rangers. Let me say at this point that these two morons were not typical of that department's employees.

They ordered me away from the dock with the van. They said no parking was permitted in that area. I tried to explain to them the circumstances of what was occurring and that if I moved away from the dock area, the family would be unable to find me, when they returned, much less get to me because of the child's handicap.

My pleas fell on deaf ears, and the two rangers said that if I didn't get out of there right away they would give me a summons. As a last resort I said, "Do you really want me to call a local newspaper? They will send a photographer down here to take a picture of you chasing away the van of a child who has asked to come to New York City as a 'wish.'"

I don't know where that idea came from. It just popped into my head.

The rangers were not moved, however. The van was.

As I pulled the van away from the spot, I thought to myself that maybe it was a good idea about calling some newspaper.

I telephoned the *Daily News*. They immediately sent a photographer sensing this was a good story. When the photographer arrived, the two rangers spotted him and his camera. They knew what was up, and quicker than you could say "smile" or "cheese please" they were gone.

They disappeared because they did not want that type of publicity. As I had thought, they weren't carrying out some specific ordinance. They were just being plain mean. I was able to get back to the right spot, and the story had a happy ending.

When I told the family what happened while they were cruising the high seas of the harbor, they were delighted. To them it was a great story. To me it was the perfect example of conflict and conquest among some New Yorkers.

In another instance, I had a family with a child, not in a wheelchair, but still with a great many difficult health problems. After giving them a full-day tour of the city, I said to them that their hotel, The Plaza, was just around the corner from a pizza place and that might be a good spot for dinner. I said good night and left.

The next morning when I was back with them for another day of touring, I got the bad news that the night before the mom's purse had been snatched in the pizza parlor by a passing piece of garbage.

I thought to myself that this family had already been given a dirty deal in life. They come to my city under such circumstances and they get robbed. Give me a break.

Not to worry, however. They told me that when they got back to the hotel, the doorman asked how their evening had been. They related what had happened, and the dad said that they had lost three hundred dollars with the purse.

Later that evening, the manager on duty at The Plaza brought the family three hundred dollars from the hotel as a gift. The family told me that if you are going to get robbed, obviously the best place in the world for it to happen is in New York City. Those were their words, not mine.

Then there was the time that I brought another "wish" child family to their hotel. As they were checking in, I noticed Robin Williams, the actor, standing in the lobby.

Well, this was my perfect opportunity to have some fun. I told the family that I wanted them to meet my good friend Robin. I said to Robin Williams that I wanted him to meet my good friends, the family. I call this my bunch-of-hot-air-in-the-lobby story.

Much to my surprise, they started talking to each other like they were really good friends. I felt quite smug in pulling off this bit. Only after a few minutes did I find out that the meeting of Robin Williams was part of the child's wish. They were all having some fun at my expense by letting me think I had arranged this little get-together.

They all left me and went up to Robin's room for a pre-arranged lunch and afternoon visit.

Let us see what we learn from this one. The family loved me having egg on my face. A cool, streetwise cabdriver who made himself look like a real sap. Not bad. The child laughed the most at my antics.

For me, I learned that a big shot like Robin Williams, who probably didn't have enough time for himself, could take an afternoon off to spend with a kid who was dealt a bad hand.

I have asked a couple of the "wish" kids to contribute to this chapter because you know that audiences love child performers. Also, I don't have to pay them anything because I promised them that this book would be turned into a movie and Tom Cruise would play one of them and Val Kilmer would play the other.

> I wished I could go to New York City and you helped make my wish come true. Before I met you I thought you were going to be just a plain old taxi driver but when I met you I thought you were a very funny guy and I knew I was going to have a good time with you. I wanted to do things like most people do like visit the Statue of Liberty, the Empire State Building, the World Trade Centre, skating in Rockefeller Centre we did all of these things and much more. You took me to see the old trains and buses at the New York Transit Authority I got in and pretended I was driving the buses you did too I have pictures of you and me. You also took me to umbertos for spaghetti my favorite, the spaghetti was good but I liked the bullet holes in the walls the most. The best part of my trip was definitely when you took me to Governors Island I got to drive the Coast Guard boat all by myself in New York Harbour I drove around the Statue of Liberty, beside a great big ship and under the Brooklyn Bridge it was so much fun I will never forget it. The worse part of my trip was going home because I didn't want to leave behind Peter Franklin. I hope you like my little letter from David Sechi.

And from another of my young friends who deserves to be in this book:

> It is quite easy to say that New York City is one of the best places to live in the world. I wouldn't have agreed with this until I visited the "Big Apple" last summer. For me, going to New York City was both an adventure and a dream come true.
>
> After talking to Peter on the telephone, I got the impression that he was your average New Yorker with the accent and everything. After meeting him, I was amazed at how confident he was about living in New York. Peter took us to virtually every possible place including some of the most dangerous places in New York. I really enjoyed going to all the tourist attractions such as the Statue of Liberty, Times Square, Empire State Building and World Trade Center. These were some highlights of my trip. However, if it wasn't for Peter, I would have never gone way up to Harlem, The Bronx, Coney Island, and to Governor's Island. On Governor's Island I got to ride on a US Coast Guard Ship where I got to see them change a buoy right in front of the Statue of Liberty. After that, I went to the marine control center where they control all the ships in New York Harbor. By far, this was one of the most memorable highlights of my trip. I have been telling you all the good parts of my trip but to be honest, there was barely anything that I disliked. The food was awesome, people were great, and I had an awesome trip. The only thing that bothered me was that Peter picked us up too early at the hotel. Just joking!
>
> Darin Yanisiew

I think I just made a mistake. In show business (and I guess the book business), they say, never let a kid get into your act.

And so as the curtain slowly falls on this chapter, I should like to say to you, dear reader, that I think you should take a minute or two at this time to think of something nice you can do for someone tomorrow.

It will be your way of paying tribute to the parents of "wish" kids all over the world. Bless them, they are real heroes.

I Say, Old Chap, Where Do I Find the Wenches?

The roads were heavy, the night misty; my conductor let his horse walk all the way, and the hour and a half extended, I verily believe, to two hours; at last he turned in his seat and said:

"You're noan so far fro' Thornfield now."[11]

All right. All right. So, I have a sense of the dramatic. My trip to the castle wasn't exactly by horse, the night wasn't misty, and it didn't take two hours.

Unless, of course, you count the time it took for me to drive to Newark Airport in New Jersey, and then take an airplane to England, and then take an underground to a train, which took me to York. Then it did take more than two hours.

I am talking about the original York, kids. I am not talking about the new one that I live in.

You, dear passenger, are with a guy who grew up hearing about a certain type of England. It was an England which had the empire on which the sun never set. It was the England that sent troops off to fight in Sudan. It was the

---

[11] *Jane Eyre*; Charlotte Bronte; Signet Classics

England where all the men wore bowler hats, and the ladies were decked out in skirt hoops.

I knew that the trains in England screamed their whistles as they went through tunnels. At least, that is what happened in Agatha Christie books. And someone was always being murdered.

London was the home of Sherlock Holmes and his sidekick, Dr. Watson. London was foggy. Arthur Conan Doyle, what a guy.

His tales about Professor Moriarity, or the one about a dog that didn't bark, are the ones that I told to my children when they were still too young to read. And when they started reading, what do you think their favorite books were?

Elementary, my dear reader—Sherlock Holmes.

And who could think of an England without conjuring up in your mind the characters from the world of Charles Dickens? His tale of a nasty old man who didn't like people or Christmas and his story about kids who were pickpockets—now, that is my kind of a city.

Have you got the point?

So, when those blokes from the British Broadcasting Corp. asked me, nay requested of me, nay beseeched me, to come and be the surprise guest keynote speaker at their annual Christmas party in Castle Howard, I was a guy with a picture of England that may have been somewhat aged.

But when I got the summons I screamed, "Bring on the wenches." To which she who must be obeyed in my house said, "I'll wench you."

And off I went.

But before I get you on the plane, let me tell you how it all came about.

One of the first radio stations in the world on which I was heard was BBC Radio York, which, of course, is in York, England.

I certainly don't mean to talk down to you, but who knows, maybe there is one among you who wouldn't realize that BBC Radio York was in York.

Sort of like not knowing who is buried in Grant's tomb here in New York City. Is it Grant?

I have found from experience it helps a good story to throw in a couple of gags here and there. If it was good enough for George Burns, it is certainly good enough for me.

Come to think of it, he used to do a little singing also. Well, I'll do that for you later.

The gentleman who was then the morning presenter for BBC Radio York and still is, is Jonathan Cowap.

Excuse me. I just have to digress again. Sorry.

You don't call BBC radio people shock jocks or disc jockeys. You call them presenters. This reminds me of the old story about three broadcasters who showed up to cover an incident at a very rich lady's house.

The butler opened the door and then proceeded to tell the lady of the house that there were two radio people and a "gentleman" from the British Broadcasting Corp.

Let me tell you, working for the bloomin' BBC is a bloomin' big deal.

Jonathan is a smart cookie for a Brit from a hick town (What can I say, that was my New York cabby wise-guy attitude then.)

He was smart enough to realize right away that he had the added bit that would delight his listeners hearing the Gabby Cabby. Jonathan would make the point that it was old York finding out what was cooking in New York.

I can assure you, however, that Jonathan of the BBC would not use the term "what was cooking."

Anyway, we had some wonderful broadcasts, and in the autumn of 1994, Jonathan asked if I would be interested in coming to England for the Christmas party.

He said that it would be kept a secret from the staff and the listeners, and the BBC would pick up the cost. He also said that they would rent a tuxedo for me so that I could be the surprise keynote speaker at the party.

Would I do it?

Was this man missing a screw? Was he not playing with a full deck? Did his elevator go up all the way? Was he a few ants short of a picnic?

You bet I'll be there.

And so the preparations were made over the next several weeks. I was given the number of a fax machine at the radio station that no one but Jonathan had access to.

The messages flew back and forth. It was as if I was in one of those great World War II movies. I was a secret agent working for the BBC. Jonathan was my contact.

You think I am nuts? You think I am some kind of Walter Mitty character? Suffice it to say that on the day I drove to Newark Airport to catch the plane, I made sure I was not being followed by constantly looking in my rearview mirror.

When I got to the British Airways counter at the airport, the wench asked me how I was going to pay for the ticket.

First big thrill of the trip was to tell her that I wasn't. I told her to examine her records, and she would find that the ticket had already been bought by the BBC.

You know, you can fly discount, you can use your bonus credits, you can grab an airline sale, but if you really want to fly nicely, have someone else pay for it.

Being the observer of life that I am, I noticed that all the female employees of British Airways looked like the actress Joan Collins. The same hair, the same makeup. The same way of talking.

Perhaps it is one of the requirements of working for British Airways.

Come to think of it. The male employees all looked like David Niven, the actor.

Watch out England. Here I come. I settled into my seat and waited for that Old World charm of the British Empire. Bring on high tea. Bring on the crumpets. Let me have some of those harrumphs they are so well known for. Toss me a few "I say, old chaps."

"Do you want something to drink? Would you like a Pepsi or a Coke?" the stewardess who also looked like Joan Collins asked. "I also have some Frito Lay potato chips or Planters peanuts," she continued.

So much for British appetizers. Let me turn on the amusement console and put in those earphones. Should be some good British in-flight entertainment.

Mmmm. Willie Nelson, Johnny Cash, Frank Sinatra, Barbra Streisand on the audio channels. And on the video? I say, old chap, it was nothing but American TV and films.

Not to worry. The plane starts in New Jersey. What would you expect? Obviously it was made ready for flight by people who live in the greater New York area.

Yes, I thought, this plane was indeed prepared for flight with food and entertainment by a bunch of people who do not wear bowlers and do not have high tea in the afternoon. It was prepared for flight by a bunch of people who drink tea only when they have a fever.

I figured that when we landed in London, I would then find my Britain. The real one.

What can I say? Maybe yes. Maybe no. There were some elements of the old Britain that I expected, but by and large my dream was shattered by the fact that there were too many McDonald's and Burger Kings in places I expected to see quaint little pubs.

Don't get me wrong. Back in New York City, my bladder depends on McDonald's and Burger King. My city has no public toilets, and most store owners are wacko when it comes to letting a noncustomer use the toilet.

McDonald's and Burger King let you use their facilities to do your business even if you aren't contributing to their business.

In other restaurants and stores, the trick is that you have to either buy something which makes you a customer or scream that you are about to pee on the floor and see if that gets you a key to the crapper.

Note the English influence with my use of the word "crapper." As my more learned readers know, Mr. Crapper, an Englishman, was the guy who invented the toilet, maybe.

Oh well, I thought, the London cabbies need a place to pee, too, so they really do have to have the McDonald's and Burger King.

Speaking of the London cabbies, I must tell you that the next Brit who gets into my cab in New York City and tells me about "the knowledge" is going to get a smack in the head from me.

In London, to be a cabdriver you have to be an apprentice for a number of years and really know the city before becoming 100 percent licensed and approved.

Contrast that to New York City where you plunk down some money for a license and poof, you are a taxi driver. Then you can say, "I don't know where Yankee Stadium is."

On the train from London to York, I sat and chatted with a couple of blokes who must have thought they were funny. I don't mean wise guys, I mean they must have thought they were funny, like in humorous.

Prior to my departure across the Big Pond (that's what they call the Atlantic Ocean), I was told to watch out for the English cooking and for English humor. Both would give you heartburn.

Here is the joke told to me. Do not hold me responsible for British humor. I am merely the messenger in this case.

The vicar in a small English town needed some guy to ring the bell in the steeple, and he advertised for such a person.

A young man applied for the job, and as the vicar was interviewing him, the guy ran across the steeple room, leaped and then smashed the side of his face into the bell, which made it ring. "Are you crazy?" asked the vicar.

Before another word could be exchanged, the young man did the same thing again. He ran across the steeple room, leaped and then smashed the side of his face into the bell, which once again made it ring. "Are you crazy?" screamed the vicar, who was getting very upset.

But before you could say "tally-ho!" the guy does it again, but this time he misses the bell and goes flying out the window and falls three stories to his death.

The vicar is beside himself with grief. He calls for the police. They show up and start to question the vicar about the unfortunate circumstances which have just transpired.

"Did you know his name?" asked the constable.

To which the vicar replied, "I didn't know his name, but his face surely rang a bell."

The train arrived in York. I was greeted at the station by Jonathan, and off we went to the hotel where I was to have a room. It was right in the middle of town.

Jonathan pointed out to me that in the area directly opposite the hotel was a place where many, many years ago, in olden times, a whole bunch of Jews were put to death. Nice story. Welcome to York.

Nobody was going to hear any "oy veys" from me in this place. And, you weren't going to catch me ordering a bagel with a schmear.

My initial alarm was unfounded. Jonathan assured me that the people of York were quite excited to finally meet their New York City cabdriver, and the chances of them burning me at some stake were quite slim. He was right. They really wined and dined me whilst I was there.

The Christmas party in Castle Howard started off with an introduction of the attendees to the keynote speaker, me. My presence was a big surprise, remember, because Jonathan had kept my invitation a secret.

I did twenty-five minutes of streetwise New York City schtick, and I had them rolling in the aisles. Even the wenches stopped serving so they could listen. I found those English wenches very sexy.

Wouldn't it be nice if this Christmas party turned into one of those great old English in-the-castle banquet feasts? Not to happen. After all, this was a British Broadcasting Corp. event, and staff members do not do anything to discredit the company or the Queen.

I was told, however, that if this had been a party of English politicians...well now, that would have been really fun.

While in England, I also got a chance to finally meet Martin Kelner on his own turf. Marty Baby (that is what I call him when we are doing a radio bit), is the host of one of the funniest shows in radio land anyplace. I would put his antics up against anyone, anytime.

He hosts a Saturday night radio show which is "live," and it is heard throughout most of England on the BBC.

So Jonathan drove me over to Leeds where Marty Baby's show has its broadcast studios.

I was taken to a real typical Englishman's dinner spot. It is called a Chinese restaurant. Talk about how we are living in one world.

After eating those typical English delicacies of chow mein and an egg roll, we went to the studio where for the next three hours I fielded questions from the audience.

There is no question the founders of the British Broadcasting Corp. were turning over in their graves.

Speaking of the founders, I also got the opportunity to visit Broadcasting House, which is the headquarters for the BBC. Situated in London, it makes you think you are in Buckingham Palace. What a joint!

Again, it was a kick to get to meet presenters that I had been talking to for years.

London will always remember the morning I did the weather and the traffic reports.

"Good morning my fellow Americans. Oops, wrong country. Here now is the London weather and traffic. We are going to have weather, and we are going to have traffic. Thanks for tuning in to the British Broadcasting Corp. this morning."

One of the bits we did that morning on the Phil Kennedy Breakfast Show was for me to telephone listeners. You can imagine the surprise of those people hearing my voice on the telephone. The same voice they had been listening to on the radio for years.

Well, as they say, the party was soon over, and it was time to go home. It isn't too easy to have been in a castle at a Christmas party in England, wearing a tuxedo, drinking champagne, and then have to change back into being a cab-driver on the streets of New York City.

But, frankly, I'd rather fight for survival on the streets being a real person, than having all that pomp and ceremony and easy living.

Bullshit.

Come on out With Your Hands Up, I Have You Surrounded

Siberia. On the banks of a broad solitary river stands a town, one of the administrative centers of Russia; in the town there is a fortress; in the fortress there is a prison. In the prison the second-class convict Rodion Raskolnikov has been confined for nine months.[12]

All right, you dirty rats. You dirty rats. Maybe you want to think of Rodion as a "second class" prisoner, but when you think of the Gabby Cabby as a prisoner, you think of me as "first class." Or else.

And don't send me to the sweet vacation land of Siberia. That is for sissies. You want to give me heavy time, you send me off to The Bronx House of Detention.

Surprise! Surprise! The author of this book, me, is an ex-con. Just like Jimmy Cagney. Just like George Raft. I mean the parts they acted in, of course.

But, I wasn't acting. I did heavy time. Well, maybe not so heavy, but it was time. To be exact it was four weeks and one day. I didn't count the minutes and seconds. Sorry about that.

---

[12] *Crime and Punishment*; Fyodor Dostoyevsky; Avon

111

I confess. I was a prisoner. I was the raw material needed for this nation's thriving growth industry. People in the slammer. As of this writing, there are oodles and oodles of prisoners being held by the New York City Department of Correction.

I love that. "Oodles" for the bad guys. "Correction" for the good guys.

If you believe that is the right word, then you probably also believe in the tooth fairy. The guards are called "correction officers." You must never ever call them "guards."

Give me a break. They were going to correct us? That is a lot of crap. Oops, excuse me for using that word. It is my old prison life coming back to me.

And as long as I am throwing around numbers here, let me point out to you, also, that as of this writing, the United States of America has more than three million people in jail. They say that almost every American family either has someone or knows someone serving time. Frankly, there would be more people incarcerated if I had my way.

My way? I would make it a felony not to give me a good tip.

By the way, I call putting people in the slammer a growth industry because it costs about $168 a day to have a prisoner in a cell in the Big Apple. For that kind of money, we could be sending the bad guys and girls off to Harvard or Princeton.

I know what you are thinking. Big deal. He was in jail once.

I confess. I confess. I was in jail once in New York. The time before I was in jail in Virginia.

Let me get the Virginia incident out of the way, first.

I had gone to visit Don Schaefer who was a talk show host on a station in Charlotte, North Carolina. The station was one of the first radio stations in the United States that I was on, and I just can't remember its call letters. Nice folks. He took me out to dinner and made me feel like a big shot.

We went to a Japanese restaurant, and I watched those southern radio people eat sushi. I didn't because once upon a time my wife and I were in a Japanese restaurant in New York City, and a rather unsettling event took place.

The man at the table next to us was eating lobster, and while he was eating the lobster, it started to move.

With that old thought in mind, I now ordered something cooked in Charlotte.

You know, it is a funny thing. It has become very "in" to eat raw fish. If you ask anyone on the groovy east side of Manhattan about it, they will tell you how delicious it is.

Delicious? How do you call something delicious that moves when you eat it? I guess I could, if I were a Klingon and my name was Worf.

Now if you look at a map, you will see that it is necessary to drive through Virginia if you are going from North Carolina to New York City.

It was a very foggy morning, about four, if I remember correctly. I was getting off the interstate in Virginia to get some gas, and I was stopped at a stop sign, hesitating before making a right turn.

All of sudden, someone is smacking on the driver's side window, screaming, "I got you. I got you." Let me tell you, that kind of sudden occurrence is enough to make you jump

RIDE FROM NORTH CAROLINA

• ⊛NYC
Smell of the oil refineries; I'm almost home!

• Free at last... kissed the good earth of Maryland

☆ Arrest, Beating, Conviction

⊛ Charlotte is down here someplace...

out of your socks. Put it another way, it was a good thing my bladder was empty.

It was a Virginia state trooper who then went on to tell me that he had been chasing me for miles.

I tried to explain to the trooper that it was not me, and if I had been evading him it was a great way to get killed, and I wasn't that stupid.

Readers, trust me on this one. Believe in me. The trooper was wrong. It wasn't my car he was after. It had to be another. Anyway, the question of my guilt or innocence really has no bearing on my jail-time story.

Now here is what Officer Putz does (remember, I told you earlier what a "putz" is. If you don't remember, you have to go back to an earlier chapter. Next time pay attention to what I write).

He grabs open the door on the driver's side and puts his hands on me. Now, let me tell you that no one, and I mean no one, ever touches me. You don't ever touch me. You don't even think of touching me. You just don't put your hands on me. I don't care who you are. You don't touch me.

Except, of course, if you are six and a half feet tall with a big gun on your belt. Then, what the heck, you can touch me.

He pulls me out of the vehicle and very roughly pushes me up against its back door and proceeds to handcuff me with my hands behind my back.

I am starting to get worried. This trooper is acting more like a wacko than a putz. A putz you can deal with. A wacko you might be in for big trouble.

As a matter of fact, I began to worry that maybe this guy wasn't really a Virginia state trooper because his behavior was so bizarre.

He drags me over to his car and pushes me in. Then, he walks back over to my car and starts to search it. He looks under the seats. He looks in the trunk. He opens up my two suitcases and looks through them.

Now, here is what I was thinking at that moment. I shall tell the trooper that he is in violation of my civil rights, and if he doesn't watch himself I will report him to the United States Department of Justice.

If found guilty of violating my civil rights, he will be dismissed from the State Police, lose his pension, and be sent to jail.

He and I were alone on a deserted stretch of an interstate in the wee hours of the morning. He had already smacked me around. I decided that the concept of civil liberties might not appeal to him at that moment.

But here's the really crazy aspect of what he did. He shoved me into his car, handcuffs on behind my back, but did not search me.

I reached down to my ankle where I keep my small pistol, and when he returned to his car, I shot him through the head.

I took the handcuff key out of his pocket, opened up the cuffs, took his money and watch, and drove off.

Whee. Had you going there for a minute, didn't I? Of course, I didn't shoot the trooper, but can you imagine how unprofessional and dangerous it was of him not to search me?

He then explained to me that he was taking me off to the slammer, but he would first call for a truck to tow my car to the impound depot. He explained that the tow trip would cost me one hundred fifty dollars.

Of course, I knew what was going on. I was being filmed for a television show starring Andy Griffith and Don Knotts. The town was probably called Mayberry.

Well, in about thirty seconds, the guy I will call Goober showed up for my car. I swear he must have been hiding along with his tow truck, behind a nearby tree. He hooks my baby up and off he goes. Kiss that sucker good-bye.

It turns out that the nearest town is Harrisonburg, Virginia, and that is where I am taken. Since it was early in the morning, the trooper had to go find a town justice.

So he puts me in a cell with a couple of gentlemen who were, as I remember, in the spirits business. They weren't the Seagram brothers. I think their names were Zeke and Efron.

They asked me a great many questions about New York City. Was it easy to rob people? Was there a market for their unique brand of designer booze?

If I had been smart that day, I would have gone into the crime business with those guys, and today I would be a rich man instead of sitting here in my cab.

You didn't realize I was writing this on a typewriter in my cab? What did you think? Did you think I was sitting at a Value Point 486 with a CTX monitor using Windows 95 and the software Word?

Her honor arrived later that morning after being telephoned by the trooper.

Isn't that what every felon wants? To be brought before some judge who has just been awakened because her local state trooper has a New York City person in the hoosgow ready for the guillotine?

As she walked into the court, I was terrified that she was going to start knitting and then start mumbling, "To the guillotine. To the guillotine."

I explained to the judge that I was the victim of mistaken identity, and if it pleased the court, I shall prove that point. I got that "if it pleases the court" from watching television.

She surprised me by saying, "Prove it." Gadzooks, that was something that never happened to Perry Mason. I couldn't prove it. It was my word against the trooper's. Who do you think a mother would believe? A guy from New York City or her son the trooper?

OK. So maybe Goober the tow guy wasn't the trooper's cousin, and maybe the judge wasn't his mother, but they sure acted like family.

I paid sixty dollars to the court. I paid one hundred fifty dollars for the tow. If you are thinking of vacationing near Harrisonburg, Virginia, just mention my name. They will probably ask you when that sucker from New York City is coming back.

As I was leaving Virginia on my trek north, I felt like one of those guys in a war movie who escapes across the border. I'll tell you this, I live for the day that trooper comes to New York City and gets into my cab.

But I already have gotten even. Boy, did I get even. I told the story of that state trooper to every radio station in Virginia. Another side benefit to doing this radio stuff. I can be a pain in the ass when I want to.

Let me see—do I have a Virginia joke? Well, how about a George Washington-type joke? He used to live in Virginia.

It is modern times in Virginia, and a father is smacking the heck out of his kid behind the woodshed. The kid is screaming, "But I told you the truth. I said I cannot lie. I cut down our cherry tree."

The father continues to beat the child. More screaming.

"Daddy, why are you hitting me? I told the truth about our cherry tree just like George Washington told the truth about his cherry tree. I know his father didn't beat George."

To which the father screamed, "His father wasn't sitting in the cherry tree when his son chopped it down."

I thought that was the end of my criminal career. It may have not been the big house, but it was still jail. Big house? Little did I know what was coming.

Take a break. Get something to eat. Come back for the next chapter, which will tell about my incarceration in New York. Oh, the things broadcasting did for me.

Up the River to the Big House

Once upon a midnight dreary, as I pondered weak and weary.[13]

No, wait a minute, that's not how it started.

In the previous chapter I wrote about how my broadcast career brought me into the prison world. I should like to make the observation that everything is a state of mind.

Even though you are in handcuffs, even though you have to pull up your trousers so they don't drag in the pee on the floor, even though a lady guard (oops, I meant to say correction officer) watches you while you make a doo-doo, you can accept it. It is merely a state of mind that determines your situation.

Remember those words well. And remember well that they are nonsense.

OK. In Harrisonburg, it was a few hours. That was all just fun after I was reasonably sure that the Virginia state

---

[13] *The Raven*; Edgar Allan Poe; Vintage Books

trooper was indeed a Virginia state trooper and was most probably not going to kill me.

I got to feel like I was Johnny Cash. You know what I mean. I made believe that I was in the big house. If only I had a metal cup to drag across the bars and yell for the "screws."

In a sense it was the dry run to the biggy. And the biggy was not too far away. Little did I know that I really was on my way to the big house.

Do you remember when I said to you before that it didn't really make any difference whether or not I was speeding and whether or not I had been evading the trooper? The point of the tale was my incarceration and the events involved with it.

Well, we got to do it again. I am now going to tell you about the four weeks and one day I spent in The Bronx House of Detention. Remember the book *Vanity of the Bonfires*? What a place.

During this period of time, my broadcasting came to an abrupt halt, but my radio stations around the world called on an almost daily basis to see how I was getting along. They called the prison. They called the state capital.

Talk show hosts were discussing that I was in the slammer. I was for that period of time probably the best-known convict in the world. If you didn't know about it, then you are not listening to your radio enough.

Wouldn't it have been nice if I could have convinced the warden to let me make those broadcasts?

"And now, live from cell block two south, The Bronx House of Detention proudly presents, The Cabby Convict."

"With today's guests, Henry the Horror, Karl the Killer, Boris the Bank Robber, and that wonderful dance team of Hookum, Bookum, and Cookum."

Dream on.

What got me into the slammer was that I was supposed to do something.

I didn't do that something. I was held in contempt of court. It wasn't my fault, because I wasn't able to do that something. But, I don't deny my guilt under the law.

However, a judge should look at all the facts and then decide what to do. To stick to the letter of the law and completely disregard the circumstances of the offense is, I believe, unfair.

But, it doesn't really make any difference what I think. The judge is in control.

Of course, if a judge is repeatedly unfair, eventually the system may catch up with her honor, and she will be removed from handling cases. Hold that thought until a little later in my story.

Upon learning by a telephone call that there was an arrest warrant for me (we are very civilized in New York City), I turned myself in at the Seventeenth Precinct on East Fifty-third Street.

A word about this precinct. It protects the midtown east area of Manhattan and as such it has all big-deal corporation headquarters, big-deal United Nations, big-deal people. Cops want to work in it. They don't want to work out in Staten Island.

By playing their cards right, they can do their time, make some really good connections, and then get a good private sector corporate security job after their retirement from the police department.

Also, they do quite well on overtime because of all the various activities that occur in this area of New York City. They are not your ordinary cops, and that is why they are the most difficult precinct to deal with as a cabdriver.

These cops know every trick in the book because they themselves are doing them already.

The mean-guy cop wanted me to be in handcuffs for the trip on the way downtown to the court. The good-gal cop thought it was unnecessary. After a brief argument, the lady cop won.

Let me talk a minute here about this combination of a male cop and a female cop. In almost all instances, New York City police officers work in pairs. It is safer for them, and it makes it easier to settle minor disputes that they have to respond to.

One cop can talk to one combatant, and the other cop can talk to the other combatant to kind of calm things down.

Now, when the idea came up about pairing male and female cops in New York City, some folks said that this would be a bad idea. There is something called "propinquity," which roughly means that when a boy and girl spend a great deal of time together, there is a good chance of some muffky fuffky.

The professional law enforcement organizations said, "Nonsense." Male and female officers would remain professional.

Well, here goes my career as a ticket-free driver on the streets of the Big Apple. I reveal to you now that some of the couples have acted like bunnies. Do you catch my drift?

OK. So, I was brought before the judge who had signed my arrest warrant.

If I thought the judge in Harrisonburg was a real hoot, I was about to find out what a really funny judge was. I asked her if I could have an attorney. She said, "No." I asked her if I could go to the bathroom. She said, "No." I asked if I could have something to eat. She said, "No."

Yeah. She was a real hoot.

In addition to being a rather unpleasant lady, she also didn't seem to know her business.

At one point during the proceedings, the judge had to call over to the city attorney for him to come to the court to explain to her how to put me in jail. Her honor didn't know how to fill out the papers of incarceration. I felt I was watching a Woody Allen movie.

I thought back to my Virginia prison days. Maybe this would be a lark. I was wrong.

Paperwork was sorted out, and two marshals arrived to take me downstairs in handcuffs and leg irons to their car. Once in the car, they advised me that if I tried to escape they would kill me. I think they were cousins to that trooper back in Virginia.

When we arrived at the back door of The Bronx House of Detention, someone had to ring the bell for us to get in. Since the two marshals were shorties, they asked me if I could reach up and ring the bell. They took off my handcuffs so that I could do it.

Can you imagine? I had to ring a bell to get into prison. Something told me that I was about to enter a very strange world.

Do you remember the movie *Stir Crazy* with Richard Pryor and Gene Wilder when they were arrested and taken to prison? In a riotous scene, because they were both so frightened, they each walked in saying to themselves, "I am bad. I am bad."

They did it with a certain bravado thinking that it would intimidate the prisoners around them. I thought when I saw the movie it was a pretty funny ploy.

That is exactly what I did. As I walked into The Bronx House of Detention surrounded by the scariest people I had ever seen in my life (and remember, I drive a cab on the streets of New York), I said over and over again, "I am bad. I am bad."

Boy, were those prisoners scared of me.

Let me stop here for a minute to tell you something that really stunk, however.

I was told in that lady judge's courtroom that a "white guy wouldn't last ten minutes in a New York City jail." Not so. There was absolutely, positively never even the hint of racial hostility while I was incarcerated.

As a matter of fact, some of the "brothers" even spoke to my wife on the telephone while I was in jail to let her know that there was absolutely nothing for her to worry about, and I would be just fine.

After I was subjected to the usual "procedures" of entering the big house, I was assigned to a cell on two south.

If you are curious as to exactly what the "procedures" were, you will enjoy my next book in which I will be giving some very vivid descriptions along with some very graphic pictures.

That book will be available for purchase, and it will be sent to your home in a plain brown wrapper. It also will be available at a store in Times Square that has the following sign on it—"Girls working their way through college."

You know, there is a law in New York state that a prisoner such as myself who was incarcerated on a civil matter, is not to be placed in contact with people who are in jail on a criminal matter.

To the right of me, in the next cell, was a guy who was fighting extradition to Louisiana in a murder case.

In the prison's library I would always sit next to a guy who had been accused of killing his girlfriend and throwing her lover out of a ten-story window.

I guess I could have announced to the guards (excuse me, correction officers) that I did not wish to associate with criminals and that legally I didn't have to. That would not have made me too popular.

What I did discover very quickly is that no inmate in a prison will ask another inmate why they are there. I hoped that they would think I was a serial killer and stay away from me.

By the way, in a conversation with Moose (the killer guy in the library), I asked him if he thought his behavior of killing one person and throwing another out the window was inappropriate. He didn't think so.

Moose was quite pleased with his behavior, and I thought to myself, well, when this guy asks me to pass him a book, I think I shall pass him a book.

Another thing. People in prison feel that they are innocent.

"I was just on the street."

What were you near?

"A men's clothing store."

Anything special about that store?

"It had a broken window."

Was anything missing?

"Yes, some of the men's clothing."

Why did the cops grab you?

"I was running away from the store."

Did you have anything in your hands?

"Yes, some of the men's clothing."

Obviously, a man who was being persecuted by the criminal justice system. I tell you here and now, if there is one thing I learned in those dark and dreary days of my hellish confinement (now that's good writing), it is that there are no guilty people in New York jails.

I used to walk around in the prison saying, "I am guilty. I am guilty." That really made them think I was a few inmates short of a prison, a few rounds short of a magazine, and a few feet short of a basketball player.

Criminals in prisons are wonderful teachers for those who wish to embark upon a life of crime. For instance, I learned that if you are going to be robbing people, it is a good idea to carry an extra set of underwear with you. It was explained to me that when arrested you are then able to take a shower and freshen up while waiting for a bail hearing.

Another tip. Try to have a small pick in your pocket. After being caught and handcuffed, you might have the opportunity to free yourself if the arresting officer is distracted for a second.

We interrupt this story for a prison joke told to me in prison.

Two convicts are planning to escape from the jail. One asks the other how they are going to make it from the roof of one building to another building to be able to escape.

The guy says that he is afraid to make the jump across.

"Not to worry," the other convict says. "I will shine a flashlight to the building and then you can walk across the beam."

The first convict replies, "What? Are you nuts? What is going to happen to me if you decide to turn off the light when I am halfway across?"

Can you imagine hearing prison jokes in a prison? Very strange, but if you think that is strange, how do you feel about watching a prison movie or a cop movie in jail?

Everyone around you is cheering for the bad guys.

And so, while I was rotting away—reading, watching television, playing basketball, and eating what I believe to be a rather well-balanced diet, my radio stations were going bananas without their regular fix of me.

When it came the day to be released, which was a Friday, I heard the captain of the guards yelling, "I don't care if the judge doesn't know how to fill out a form properly or not, get him out of here."

The captain came over to me and said, "Look, this judge didn't know how to put you in here. She doesn't know how to get you out. I am letting you go, but if this has to be redone, I want you back here on Monday."

Yeah. Sure. Lots of luck.

And here is a little footnote to this story. Sometime after my incarceration, a great many lawyers in the City of New York signed a petition asking that this dreadful lady judge be removed from hearing cases because of the great number of her bad decisions. She was.

You see, one of the wonderful things about New York City is that no matter what goes wrong, eventually it gets straightened out, and the good wins.

I am back on the streets of New York City driving my yellow mobile conveyance lounge and eating a bagel with a schmear.

This episode and the one in Virginia have really helped me to understand the criminal mind. Lady judges.

And an anonymous letter to the Corrections Department has suggested that their short marshals get lifts in their shoes to make them taller.

ANOTHER CASE CLOSED BY THE NEW YORK CITY CRIMINAL JUSTICE SYSTEM.

Someday, I Am Going to Write a Book

Serene was a word you could put to Brooklyn, New York. Especially in the summer of 1912. Somber, as a word, was better. But it did not apply to Williamsburg, Brooklyn. Prairie was lovely and Shenandoah had a beauty. Serene was the only word for it, especially on a Saturday afternoon in summer.[14]

My young Saturday afternoons in New York City, which were somewhat later than 1912, were also very serene, but more important, they were the days that helped me become the consummate observer of New York City life.

There I did it. I have always wanted to write a paragraph that said I was the "consummate" something or other. I think it is a very posh way of claiming to be an expert on a particular topic.

And the reason I also love that word is that one of my most pleasant recollections of growing up in this city was an almost daily trip that we teenagers made to a local Jewish delicatessen to get some snacks.

---

[14] *A Tree Grows In Brooklyn*; Betty Smith; Harper & Row

Come to think of it, I don't know if the word "snacks" is quite appropriate to what we used to eat. Perhaps it would be better classified as a banquet fit for King Henry VIII. Wouldn't it be great to have a teenage stomach that never seems to add weight to your frame?

Today's teenagers hang out in malls. Poor babies. They will never know what a kick it is to hang out in a store that is actually owned by the person who is there and not by some corporation at the other end of the country.

You folks who grew up in small towns also understand exactly what I mean. You didn't hang out in a mall either. You hung out in the local store owned by a real person.

The really-owned-by-someone store has a personality, and you go there for something more than just the food. Ask any regular why he always eats at a particular place.

Have I now made the point, or do I have to continue to beat this thought to death?

Anyway, getting back to the word "consummate," I will now connect it to that Jewish delicatessen. (Talk about eventually getting to the heart of a story, but I know you are enjoying reading this as much as I am enjoying writing it.)

One of the waiters there would always ask if you wanted the "consummate" or the chicken noodle soup? It was one of my first wonderful introductions to finding out that somehow folks in the Big Apple were, how can I best put this, unusual in behavior and speech. Of course, he meant "consommé."

I have been watching New Yorkers, listening to them, studying them, ever since those delicatessen days.

When it came time for me to order, I would always get something called a chicken salami sandwich on rye with a side order of french fries and a soft drink. My friend Irving would order the same thing, only he would always order coleslaw and put it on the sandwich instead of eating it on the side.

A continuing problem with Irving and his sandwich creation was that every time he would laugh about something, huge chunks of chicken salami and coleslaw would fly across the table at the person who was sitting opposite to him.

Unfortunately, that was me, because for reasons only the good Lord might know, we always sat in the same chairs, day after day, week after week, month after month.

You had to be very careful about saying something at that table without thinking about it first. Say something that would excite Irving and splat, you would be covered with food.

I contend here and now that if you want to teach people how to think about what they are about to say before saying it, have them sit opposite Irving in a Jewish delicatessen.

Talking of spit, I have never forgotten the day when another teenage friend, Jerry, spit on my Ted Williams autograph. Ted Williams was a guy who played for a team called the Boston Red Sox, which, if I remember correctly, played in an enemy city called Boston.

Jerry knew that at that time a New York kid had to root for the New York Yankees baseball team, which meant he had to spit on a Ted Williams autograph if he saw one.

That is exactly why I had my Uncle Jack, who was the world's leading authority on sports, make up a phony Ted Williams autograph so that I could aggravate Jerry.

I knew if Jerry saw that autograph, he would make an attack on it. Jerry didn't disappoint me. He spit once. He spit twice. He spit three times. Now that is what I call a New York spitter.

After the great rains ended from his smirking mouth, I told my buddy Jerry that the autograph belonged to my Uncle Jack and that I expected to get a financial settlement for him since the ink was now smudged on the paper.

I guess the fact that I told Jerry that the autograph actually was owned by an adult put him into a panic. He gave me five dollars for the injustice to Ted Williams. Naturally, I used that five bucks for a chicken salami sandwich with a side order of french fries and a soft drink.

These types of incidents were the basic training for my eventual career choice.

What better place in the world is there to have a daily diet of funny people—strange people, crazy stories—than in the driver's seat of a New York City taxicab?

What you see and hear in the Big Apple is not something that you will see and hear in Idaho. This is why more people from Idaho come to New York City than vice versa.

Vice versa. I like that expression also. I think maybe they named a house of ill repute that. It was on Fourteenth Street. Or maybe I am thinking of Laverne's House of Pleasure. I don't know. Sometimes I just forget things.

This digression reminds me of the time the Democrats held their convention in New York City in 1992.

The city was filled with politicians, and many of them would get into my cab and ask, "Where can you go for a good time?"

I don't know what kind of a readership I am dealing with, but to be on the safe side, I want to explain to you that that question means the passenger wanted to have "fun" with another person. At that time, it was a person of the opposite sex. Now things have changed, and it is far more complicated.

Then it was easy. I knew the boys wanted girls. These days, I have to kind of figure out exactly what the passenger means. Does he want a girl? Does he want a boy?

Oy vey! Maybe he wants me.

Don't get me wrong. Democrats are not more hot to trot than Republicans. It was that they just happened to be holding their convention in New York City. I don't drive a cab in Houston, Texas, where the Republicans had their convention that year.

I am sure that the Democrats who asked me that question so often in those few days were merely doing some type of government research. It was probably a heavily funded program created to do a feasibility study on whether or not "fun" was something you should pay for.

Did I ever tell you the story about the Democrat whose wife died, and before her body was even cold he was making passionate love to the household hired help?

Several of his friends who were with him at the funeral were taken aback when upon their return to his house, they accidentally walked into the Democrat's bedroom and found him doing muffky fuffky with the maid.

"My goodness," one of his friends said. "Have you no respect for the dead? Your wife is hardly settled in the ground, and we find you doing this with the maid."

Without missing a beat (if you catch my drift), the recently designated widower responded, "In my grief I don't know what I am doing."

You must admit that it was quite clever the way I moved my story from the Democratic Convention in New York City to a joke. I made the main character in the joke a "Democrat" merely for the transition. I have only done twelve chapters before this, but you got to admit, I am starting to get good at it.

Let us take a minute now for me to explain to you what a "shabbos door" or a "shabbos elevator" is. It is necessary for you to know this to understand my next true tale.

On the west side of Manhattan, we have many orthodox Jewish people. Some of them are so religious that on Saturday (their Sabbath and day of rest), they will not answer the telephone, ride a bus, open a door, or ride in an elevator.

When they say "day of rest," they really do mean resting. They will do nothing at all other than studying the bible or praying. This is something which dates back thousands of years, and it is in a sense showing the ultimate respect to the good Lord.

But there are some necessities that can't be put aside in the modern world. You can't have an eighty-year-old orthodox Jewish person with a heart condition walking up thirty-five flights of stairs to his apartment even if it is the Sabbath.

So you make one particular elevator in the building, the "shabbos elevator." It is kind of OK to use this elevator on a Saturday. Call it a dispensation.

The same would hold true for a "shabbos door." This would be, for instance, one of the self-opening, electric-eye doors at the entrance to an apartment house. It would be designated as the "shabbos door," and even though it was mechanical, it would be all right for the orthodox to use.

Remember, religion is a question of faith. Don't ever look for logic.

OK. So now that you understand all of this, I can tell my story.

This guy gets into my taxi on the West Side, and we go about a block or two when I stop for a red light. I look in the rearview mirror and I don't see him.

I turn to get a better look, and I see that he is laying down on the backseat of the cab.

"Are you dead?" I ask.

"No," he replies, "I am hiding from my rabbi."

"Hiding from your rabbi?" I continue my interrogation.

The passenger explains that he is an orthodox Jewish person, and he really shouldn't be riding in a cab on a Saturday. We are just going past his rabbi, he explained, who is out on the sidewalk, and he didn't want his religious leader to see him in the cab.

It was quite obvious to me that my passenger was really worried about the ramifications of what he was doing, but he indicated that he was in a rush to get from one side of town to the other and had to risk the wrath of not only his rabbi but also that of the good Lord.

Listen to me. Being a good cabdriver means also being able to calm passengers who are upset. You do that because you are decent and care for your fellow humans.

You also do it because, maybe, you will get a good tip.

Thus, I explained to my passenger, trying very hard to sound as ecumenical as possible, that there was no need for him to worry. The cab he was in had been recently designated the New York City "Shabbos Taxi," and as such it was approved for riding therein by all agencies issuing approval for such things.

Listen, reader, don't give me any holier-than-thou stuff at this point. I wasn't making fun of his religion. I was trying to be a good guy and bring him a little peace of mind.

His anxiety was relieved because he believed my silly declaration, and I thought to myself that my late mother, a very funny lady with a wonderful sense of humor, would have enjoyed that story.

After the man got out of the cab and walked away, I opened the window, leaned out of the taxi, looked up at the sky, and yelled at the top of my lungs, "Ma, that one was for you."

Not one person even turned to look at me. What do you think? That it is unusual for cabdrivers on the streets of New York City to lean out their windows and yell? Nah, we do it all the time.

Speaking of Jewish people, let me give you another story. Don't worry, the one after this one will be concerning gentiles. Right now I am on a Jewish roll, and I don't mean a bagel.

OK. I gave you a short course about the shabbos door. Now, I got to explain about "Jewish guilt" before I tell my next true tale.

Making your kids feel guilty about everything is the primary job of a Jewish mother. They probably go to some secret school someplace where they are taught the art. Everything is a warning. Everything is doom. Have guilt. It is good for you to have guilt.

Having observed this phenomenon for many years and being on the receiving end of it from time to time, I know how to dish it out, also.

If you don't button the top button of your coat, you will die of pneumonia.

If you sit on a cold park bench, you will get piles.

If you sit too close to the television screen, you will go blind. (This is not to be confused with the other sure path to blindness, which has something to do with unilateral sex.)

This lady, her husband, and her two kids get into my taxi on Central Park South and give me a destination of Ninety-sixth Street and Park Avenue. I know immediately that they are Jewish people.

How do I know such a thing? Oy vey! You don't think I can't recognize one of those people when I see them? You must be a schlimazel.

I pull away from the curb, and, frankly, I missed turning into Central Park, which would have been the quickest way to our destination. Really, it was an honest mistake, I wasn't looking to get a long ride and a big fare out of this.

If you don't believe me, I don't really care. If after all these chapters you don't feel like my friend who trusts me, then who wants you? Did I need you to buy this book? Don't do me any favors.

All the way, block after block, street after street, the husband is giving me the business. Over and over, I hear, "He should have taken the park."

He must have said it a hundred times. I wanted to crack him in the head.

Finally, we get to the destination, and I figure now he is going to get it from me.

He starts to pay me and offers a tip besides. I tell him that I cannot take the money because as a New York City taxi driver I have done a poor job, and I am ashamed.

With that statement, the game was afoot. The wife told me that there was no need for me to be ashamed and that I had probably done the best job that I could. She told me to take the money.

I said I couldn't. I was too ashamed.

She began to beg. She begged some more.

I still refused to take the money.

She asked how my family would survive if I didn't take money from passengers.

I explained that I do take money from passengers, but in this case I was too ashamed, and I knew that my family would rather go hungry than have me take the money. By the way, I told her that my wife wasn't doing too well, and the children had been sick a great deal recently.

By this time, she is begging me to take the money, so I finally figure enough is enough. I take it.

What happened next is something I could have bet a gazillion dollars on. As they walked away from the cab, I heard the husband softly say to his wife, "He should have taken the park. He should have taken the park." He said it over and over, and I guess he is still saying it.

And now, here, as promised, is my next true story, which, as I promised you, would not be about Jewish people. These two gentiles named Rabinowitz and Rubinstein. Only kidding. Read on.

I picked up this cute girl in lower Manhattan who gave me as the destination a theater in Times Square. How did I know she was cute? How did I know she was really, really cute?

Once again, based on my years of observation of people in New York City, once again based on my natural ability to know and understand the vocations of people, once again I got eyes, don't I?

As we are moving through traffic at the usual pace of a snail, I start to hear strange noises from the backseat of the cab. I hear "oooh." I hear "aaah." I hear "eeeh."

This is great, I am thinking. Something fantastic is happening, and maybe I can play in the game, also.

My problem is that I cannot see what she is doing because we now have partitions in our taxis to separate me from you so that you can't rob me. This, of course, presumes that you are a moron crook who doesn't realize that all you have to do is to tell me that you will shoot your bullet through the back of my seat if I don't give you the money.

The wonderful sounds from my cute passenger continue for the duration of the ride. Maybe there is someone else in the backseat with her?

Anyway, we get to our destination, and she pays me and gets out. As she walks away, I realize what has happened. She is wearing a different set of clothing than the one she had on when she got into the cab.

She had changed what she was wearing while in the backseat of my taxi, and I didn't get to see a thing because of a partition which is supposed to save my life.

Those partitions are really dangerous. Knowing that you missed seeing a cute girl in her underwear in the backseat of your cab could actually give you a heart attack.

It is enough already. Chapter is over.

Quiet on the Set, I Said,
Quiet on the Set, Darn It

Alice was beginning to get very tired of sitting by her sister on the bank, when suddenly a White Rabbit with pink eyes ran close by her. She ran across a field after it, and was just in time to see it pop down a large rabbit-hole.[15]

The child soon found herself tumbling down that hole into a place called "Wonderland." A different type of a place. A weird place. A world with strange characters.

She had probably fallen into the world of American television. A different type of a place. A weird place. A world with strange characters.

Tanya and I were sitting in the Market Diner. I don't remember what she had for breakfast. I know I must have had my usual bagel with a schmear.

Not a bad-looking babe. I stared into her eyes, which were two pools of temptation. Her lips were pursed as if to say, "Kiss me." Her hair glistened in the morning sun that peeked its way into the diner.

---

[15] *Alice in Wonderland*; Lewis Carrol; Delacorte Press

"Lamby-pie," she said to me. "Let me put you on television."

My goodness! My palms were filled with sweat.

I took her into my arms and whispered, "Tanya, I am yours. I belong to CBS now. Take me."

OK. So I took a little literary license here. This is television I am talking about, sweetheart, and because of that, babe, well, you got to add a little schmaltz to the story, honey.

Instant explanation. Schmaltz is chicken fat in Yiddish. I guess the best definition for the way I am using it is to give a bunch of added fat to the adventure. Is the fat necessary? It sure is, if you want good television ratings.

The scene with Tanya really didn't take place that way, but if I knew then what I know now about dealing with people in the television industry, it should have.

Now, I would have had my people meet with her people, and her people would have met with my people, and they would have then met again for a business breakfast and then they would have crunched some numbers.

But those were those days, and today is today. There were no such meetings. The next person I got to meet in the television world was Dan-CBS.

For reasons that were never explained to me and are probably considered top secret deep in the Columbia Broadcasting System's headquarters, it took me fourteen months to get from Tanya to Dan-CBS.

Tanya was an assistant producer, and she thought it would be quite nice to do a television piece about me and my cab driving and my broadcasts. It was apparent that no one paid any attention to her at CBS until a startling event occurred.

There was an article about me in the *National Enquirer*, and there was an article about me in *The Wall Street Journal*. What was startling?

They both appeared on the same day. That is a dream of every public relations person in the United States. Pull off that kind of a stunt. As a matter of fact, I bet every phone of every public relations person was ringing off the desk from clients who wanted to know why that couldn't be done for them?

Right after the two articles appeared, Tanya telephoned me and told me that CBS decided that they wanted to do a profile of me. I guess I was now really "hot." It was to be done on a show called *Eye to Eye,* and the host of that show was a lady named Connie Chung.

I was told that this was a wonderful opportunity for me to get famous. You see, Connie Chung's show had fourteen million viewers each week.

Wow. I was really impressed. I had three hundred million listeners in seventy-one countries. Boy, now I was going to be famous. Give me a break.

The producer of the segment was to be Dan-CBS. Tanya didn't put it that way, but to me Dan-CBS will always be Dan-CBS.

Maybe that is because he always introduced himself as, "I am Dan-CBS." I bet that is the way he proposed to his wife. "Darling, I am Dan-CBS. Will you marry me?"

"Officer, you can't give me a summons. I am Dan-CBS."

"Please open the kitchen for us, we are hungry. I am Dan-CBS."

I told Tanya that I would love to become famous, but I would first like to spend some time with Dan-CBS in my cab so that I could be sure he had a feel for exactly what I was doing.

That was important for me. I knew what I was doing was great fun for me, and I knew that people would enjoy the story if it was shown in the right way.

I picked up Dan-CBS at his apartment building early one morning. He and I then spent a few hours with him sitting in the front seat of the cab.

The immediate problem I thought I would have would be explaining to passengers who this unexpected person was. Frankly, I thought the average New Yorker would not get into a cab if there was an unidentified person sitting next to the driver.

Why was he there? Who was he?

These were questions, I thought, that would have to be answered to the wary passenger.

Not quite. Just another reason New Yorkers are unusual. In the three hours he was with me, not one single passenger hesitated about getting into the cab, and not one was even interested in asking who Dan-CBS was.

Finally out of exasperation I started offering information.

He is the chairman of the Taxi and Limousine Commission checking up on one of his drivers.

He is a Russian seeking asylum, but unknown to him, as soon as I let you out of the cab, I am taking him back to the Russian Embassy for repatriation to his country.

He is Gene Kelly's son, and he is researching for the new movie, *On The Town, Two.*

He is the owner of the cab, but he doesn't trust me, and so for years he rides in the front seat counting the cash.

No problem. As far as the average New Yorker is concerned, if that's your story, that's your story. No big deal.

Dan-CBS was happy with what he saw and heard and decided that he would do the show. He told me that the Connie Chung show had eighteen million viewers.

I remembered that Tanya had told me fourteen million, so I told Dan-CBS that I had six hundred million listeners.

He said that maybe *Eye to Eye* had nineteen million viewers.

I said that I probably had seven hundred million listeners.

I waited for him to say twenty million. If he did, I would have raised my numbers to eight hundred million.

He didn't. Score one for the cabdriver.

About a week or so later, I was asked to show up at the corner of Fortieth Street and Park Avenue for the first day's shooting. If I remember correctly, Dan-CBS wanted to have Grand Central Station in the background for that shot.

Although I wasn't told to, I brought along my taxicab. My instincts told me that there was a probability that it might be helpful to have it.

Dan-CBS was there. Tanya was there. And they introduced me to Edward Caraballo, a very big deal video man who had won four Emmys. Nice guy.

It was made very clear by Dan-CBS to me that day and the days that followed that no input was wanted from me. After all, what could I possibly know about the subject which was about to put on video?

To be fair, I must tell you, however, Dan-CBS did a remarkable job, I think, in capturing what I was doing. So maybe he was right.

What really knocked my socks off was that he arranged for video crews in Johannesburg, Hong Kong, and London to walk the streets asking people if they listened to the Gabby Cabby. He included those bits in the finished piece.

Can you imagine what that must have cost CBS?

I think even Dan-CBS was surprised as to how well known I was. Gee, wouldn't it have been fun if they had asked those same people in the streets of those cities whether or not they knew of Connie Chung?

Connie who?

By the way, I never got to meet her at all. The way they work these things it seems, is that the hosts just kind of start and end the show. The producers, the camerapeople, and maybe a reporter if there is one, actually go out on the story.

Based on that adventure and my subsequent encounters with the television industry, it is apparent to me that the industry is riding on the coattails of the people who actually do the work, the cameramen, the sound people, the stagehands, etc. I never saw a camerawoman, but I guess there must be some.

One of the things that Dan-CBS wanted to do was to get some scenes of me driving my yellow mobile conveyance lounge up to Schenectady, New York, about 150 miles north, where I was set to do some cohosting on a station called WGY.

As we drove north on the New York State Thruway, my cab was followed by the CBS car. We started to attract quite a bit of attention.

Remember, a New York City cab is probably the most known vehicle in the world, thanks to Hollywood movies and New York City's television shows. Folks don't expect to see one of our cabs outside of the Big Apple.

I was in seventh heaven. I was able to ham it up. At each tollbooth, I would ask the toll collector if this was the way "TO" New York City. They, of course, would immediately tell me that I was heading "TO" Canada and then give me details as to how I should be heading south and not north.

When we would stop at a highway rest stop, I would shout to people who were there, "Who ordered the cab?" My explanation to people who had the courage to ask me if I was for real was, "Someone called from this rest stop, and I came to get them."

I must tell you I was amazed at the number of people who would come over to look at a real live New York City taxi driver and his cab.

Well, we got into Schenectady, but we just couldn't find the radio station from the directions we had been given. So I did what was natural. I hailed a passing cab and told him that Dan-CBS would pay him to lead us to WGY. He did and Dan-CBS did.

As a guest cohost with Tom Parker, the radio station's program director, I was able to have the time to tell some of my true tales in their entirety. This was something that was not always possible on the usual short reports that I generally did for that station.

I usually, by the way, would do bits with Don Weeks, who is the regular morning talk show host. I think Mr. Parker locked Don in a closet while the CBS people were there so that he could be on national television. Only kidding. Don was away on vacation and will probably never forgive me for the bad timing.

The WGY audience are people who live in upstate New York and as such have a certain love/hate relationship with New York City. They look upon us as somewhat crazy and erroneously believe that we cost them money. To the contrary, New York City contributes far more money to the state then they give to us. My mayor asked me to point that out to my readers in exchange for his promise that I would get no traffic summons from the police for six months.

I think my best story that morning was the one about the time I picked up a very famous person on East End Avenue and drove him nuts, I think.

You know, when you are driving a cab, you should keep the doors locked. You just don't want some person to unexpectedly get into the taxi. Even if the person means no harm, it is startling to have someone suddenly be there.

I had stopped for a red light, and I had forgotten to lock the doors. All of a sudden I heard in a somewhat heavy German accent, "This is a very clean taxi."

I thought to myself—had I picked up Arnold Schwarzenegger?

Turning around, I found myself looking square into the face of Henry Kissinger. If I have to tell you who he is, then you have been living on another planet.

He gave me his desired destination along with the route he wanted. Ach du lieber, I thought, this guy really is organized. What can I do to have some fun?

I know.

"You look very familiar to me," I said.

"Jawhol," he replied.

Well, he didn't really say "jawhol," but since I have to distinguish between what he said and what I said, I will now take my usual literary license.

One fast thought. Is this literary license I have heard about so much something you can get like a taxi driver's license? I guess you plunk down sixty dollars once a year and then you can do anything in a book you want to do.

"Sir, you look like familiar to me?"

"Jawhol."

"Didn't you play the part of the doctor on the soap opera *General Hospital*?"

"Nein, I did not," he almost shouted.

I knew he was annoyed that I didn't seem to know who he really was, so I pursued this line of questioning. "Did you ever play center field for the Boston Red Sox?"

Now he really was starting to become agitated. I knew I was in the homestretch now.

I said, "Oh, I know who you are. You used to be in the government."

In the rearview mirror I saw that he was finally starting to loosen up a bit, and that is when I crushed him with, "You are Richard Nixon."

"Nein, you dumkopf, I vas not and I am not ever the Richard Nixon." (Remember, I am reciting his words as best I can remember. He may not have called me a "dumkopf," but I am sure he was thinking it.)

He left the taxi quite disgruntled. His day was ruined. Mine was complete.

So, Henry, now you know that I knew who you were.

Gotcha!

By the way, Henry, if you aren't too angry at me, why not buy some more copies of this book and give them out to friends?

After that morning show at WGY was over, we returned to New York City back down the thruway. I had a walkie-talkie in the cab, and Dan-CBS had one in the other vehicle so that he could stay in touch with me. I also had a small TV camera in my cab that was recording the taxi meter to show how much this ride would cost if there really was a passenger with me.

I figured in the back of my mind that Dan-CBS would see that I got that money from CBS.

The job is on the way.

The check is in the mail.

I will marry you in the morning.

The rest is history. After the show aired, I got telephone calls from every producer there is offering to give me my own television show. My wife and I decided, however, that I should just stay a cabdriver and refuse all the big money offers.

We want to stay down in the trenches with you common folks and struggle to pay our bills each month. That is why I still drive the cab twelve hours a day.

Do we have time for one final joke in this chapter? It is one that I told at WGY that day. We do? Thanks. Here it is.

The Native American chief (I don't want to offend any one group unless I can offend everyone equally) had three sons.

Rain In The Face.

Brave Before Buffalo.

Falling Rocks.

Now the chief said to his three sons, "You must go out into the forest to prove your manhood and the right to sit in the council by bringing me back the hide of a wild boar."

The three sons were gone for several weeks, and one day Rain In The Face returned with the hide of wild boar, and the chief was filled with much pride.

Several days later, Brave Before Buffalo also returned with a hide of the wild boar, and the chief was filled with much pride.

But the third son was nowhere to be seen. He was never heard from again. The chief was filled with grief for the rest of his life. In his anguish, he decided that he must do something. He must ask the people of this continent to look for his missing son.

And that, dear passengers, is why all over this nation, from sea to shining sea, you will see signs on the highways and the byways saying,

"Watch Out For Falling Rocks."

Show Your
New York
Attitude

with fun, high quality merchandise from the Gabby Cabby. Both the T-shirt and ball cap are 100% cotton and feature the Gabby Cabby logo. Yo! Order today!

Item	Description	Price	Quantity	Total price
T-shirt	X/L only, 6 color logo	$18.99		
Ball cap	Yellow with black bill	$19.99		
Subtotal				
6% sales tax for Connecticut orders only.				
Shipping and handling via UPS for all orders				$8.00
Total				
Send check or money order only. Allow 6 weeks for delivery.				

Along with quantity and cost information above, please include name, complete shipping address and phone number.

Mail your order to:
Gabby Cabby
GO Management
361-4 Post Road West, Suite 260
Westport, CT 06880